she
minds
her own
business

KRYSTEL STACEY

she minds her own business

KRYSTEL STACEY

MERACK PUBLISHING

Published and distributed by Merack Publishing.
Author Photographs by Charissa Magno

Library of Congress Control Number:
Stacey, Krystel, 1986 -
She Minds Her Own Business
ISBN: 978-1-949635-29-4 Hardcover
        978-1-949635-30-0 Paperback
        978-1-949635-31-7 eBook

dedication

Dedicated to my Ever Grayce

My dearest daughter, Everthyne, you are my northern star,
light of my life, and I can't wait to see what God has planned
for you and your bright future.

Have courage, be kind and adventurous, ride Dumbo, wander
the streets of Paris, mind your own business, and most of all,
follow your heart. Shine my darling.

"Let all that you do be done in love"
1 Corinthians 16:14

contents

introduction

"She" is an entrepreneur who designed her life and loved every inch of it. She was not worried about what "they" were doing or how they defined success. She didn't listen to what they had to say because she wasn't doing it for "them." She set her own standards and priorities. She pursued her goals and lived life to its fullest potential. She kept her head in the clouds and her feet on the ground. She stayed focused on the *joie de vivre,* celebrating the joy of life with each and every tiny victory.

My hope is that by the end of this book, "she" is *you.* In the pages that follow, I will walk you through how I became this woman— and how you can become her too.

The vision for this book began after spending eight spectacular days in France. I followed my heart to Paris and then headed to the châteaus in the Loire Valley. I spent time regrouping, resetting, and exploring not only the world around me, but my own soul. I gave myself a chance to examine my own life objectively, looking from the outside in at the life I had, the choices I had made and the circumstances that had brought me to where I was. Then I dug deep down to decide what I truly wanted for my future.

This time alone was important. Being able to wander off on my own in France, instead of my usual default setting as leader of the pack. This gave me the space to process, and I had some life changing moments. With no destination in mind, I explored the streets of Saint-Germain, stumbled across the most glorious sunset while standing on the bridge at Pont au Change, and listened to the most spectacular concert at Sainte-Chapelle—not just with my ears, but with my heart. Breathing deeply, I roamed through the royal gardens of Versailles and drank a whole glass of freshly squeezed orange juice directly from a tree in Marie Antoinette's garden. I felt small—yet somehow powerful—standing next to the Eiffel Tower. Adventuring through château after château and imagining how different life there must be from my own life back in California put things into perspective. It felt as though I was seeing myself from a distance. This view would prove to be essential to my new found vision.

Only in stepping back to evaluate myself was I able to clear my thoughts and reach a critical *aha!* moment. (Of course, eating crêpes, cake, and croques monsieurs helped.)

At this point in my business and in my life, what I most needed was *to mind my own business*. To stop worrying about what everyone around me was doing and focus on the life I was meant to lead. Only then could I decide what I wanted, how I wanted to feel each day, and then make it happen.

As soon as I stopped seeking approval and attempting to replicate others' business models is when I grew the most. I felt like a different person. I asked myself two simple questions: *What do you want your life to look like? How are you going to get there?*

In attempting to answer those questions, I realized *I* get to design my life. *I'm* the one who adds richness and detail, creating a unique garment stitched together from my insights and experiences—a custom fit that is the life I choose. When we step outside our usual routines and allow ourselves to dream, we actually become more grounded. I decided to repeat this process every six months in order to evaluate what I want for my life next.

Here's the thing: you get to create the blueprint for the life you're building. With my background in fashion, wedding planning, and a love for France, I began to see this process in much the same way as making a "couture gown" that fits you like a glove.

---

couture

cou·ture/ko͞oˈto͞o(ə)r/

noun

1. the design and manufacture of fashionable clothes to a client's specific requirements and measurements.

2. fashionable made-to-measure clothes.
"Maria's couture gown was designed specifically for her by a renowned designer."

— Merriam-Webster Dictionary

In the same way that with Couture fashion you aren't just buying a dress off the rack, in life you aren't just settling for what's been given to you, either. You are creating something that is custom made, just for you. You get to choose the shape, fabric, thread, buttons, trim, and adornments of your "gown." With so much ready-to-wear at our fingertips, we often forget about the design, about taking a moment to choose. This is not just about our clothing. We can customize our *life!* Circumstances outside of our control will happen, but ultimately, it's up to us to decide how we will respond to them. Together, we will work through problems, not around them, which will make us feel more in control and confident as other issues arise.

I have lovingly created this book and the accompanying *OWN IT* workbook in order to help you design your own haute couture life, stitch by stitch. The book is a collection of learned ideas, systems, and thoughts that have helped me *mind my own business.* The workbook is your "France"—a place to explore and record your own thoughts and dreams. I highly recommend writing down your ideas in order to process what you've read and learned. The *OWN IT* workbook is designed to be a comprehensive companion guide and I truly believe it to be a worthwhile asset that will not only save you time, but allow you to dig deep into your own experiences, dreams and goals.

> *"I felt the workbook was an invaluable resource to have alongside the book. When I was having a hard time digging deeper into myself, the workbook helped to methodically get those answers to the surface. It was also a nice way to have everything in one place to look back on!"*
>
> *- Lauren Miller, entrepreneur and graphic designer*

I see the world, not always as it is, but how it should be! I see potential everywhere, with beauty around every corner, and I tend to find the positive even in times of great adversity.

Although I led a charmed and privileged childhood, I also dealt with my share of challenges. As beautiful as life can be, it also presents trials none of us could prepare for. I quickly came to understand that life comes with its own set of complications. Because I have lived through these challenges I desire *the best*, not only for myself but for those around me. I often find I want more for others than what they want for themselves. It has taken time to fully understand that I cannot realistically fulfill that desire, no matter how much I push people or try to make them see what they *could* have. If they don't want it, it's not going to happen.

So, my question for you is: *Do you want it?* Do you want to mind your own business, take control, and design a life you love? An affirmative answer is your beginning to getting the most out of this book.

After speaking on many stages, coaching business owners, and helping dear friends with life choices, I have come to realize I can best help others with their businesses when I am *minding my own business and speaking vision.*

This allows me to help guide you to envision your life in a new light, from a different angle, and to help you discover what's possible. I can show you what it will look like if you take the leap. To put that in context, I'll share with you the steps I took to get to where I am in my own life and business journey.

As a vision strategist I guide brands, entrepreneurs, and dreamers to envision a future of possibility, and then achieve it. Through a framework I've developed over ten years growing multiple businesses, I've equipped individuals and business leaders like yourself to attain dreams they once wouldn't even say out loud. Presenting this framework in book form allows me to reach you, dear reader, and motivate you in your dreams. The following pages are brimming with systems, processes, opportunity and vision for your life, and I invite you to run, jump, and dance to the fullest with this gift!

If you follow the processes through, you'll gain a new tool for shaping your future, because you will discover a vision for yourself. Once you begin to believe in that vision, and have confidence that it is possible, you will start to *own it* and to truly mind your business. That's when the magic happens.

This is how it happened for me. My business journey really began as a wedding planner and designer. I started by helping people expand on their vision for their wedding—showing them what the ceremony and reception *could* be, instead of just going with what they thought they wanted. Societal pressure and comfort with the status quo too often dulls our imaginations. Working on weddings helped me put the shine back into human potential.

But planning weddings as a standalone offering limited what I could give to people. Why couldn't they apply that same bold vision to their everyday lives: to their relationships, to their professional endeavors? I decided to branch out. My wedding planning business, Couture Events, is comprised of an incredible team of coordinators. I hold retreats for our team every six months, and last year we decided to open up the retreats to all women entrepreneurs who wanted help taking their businesses to the next level and celebrating every tiny victory. This became "Confetti Conference"—a space where we could focus on mindful growth and goal setting. From this grew my own passion for helping other women take control and mind their own businesses.

This book is the natural next step toward reaching even more women—to help them create a life they love and feel good in. I found that it starts with taking the reins and forgetting about how others see you or what they expect you to do. Instead of striving to be what the world suggested, I created a role for myself that embraces who I am at my core. This book is about discovering who you are at your core and proclaiming it to the world. I wish I would have had this book when I started my business, to use as a roadmap to guide and help me discover what I really wanted for my life and business and then give me the steps to achieve it.

I believe in you. When we all embrace excellence, we lift each other up. This book invites you to join that club and rise. I want you to see yourself and your business in the best light, reflecting your best self.

You were made for brilliance, darling. Step into it.

With my vision and firm belief in you, you'll have the power to achieve your potential! You can use some of the same tools I did to get ahead.

Think of the following pages as a sewing basket of the things you will need to know if you are going to *mind your own business*. Note: it's *your* business. It is up to you to use the tools, resources, and guidance I pass along and make them your own. *You* determine how your life will flourish, transform, and become your own. You will need to take the time to make the dress exactly as you'd like it... but you will love walking in the couture gown that is your life once you do.

Let's get started.

CHAPTER N⁰ 1

DESIGNING YOUR COUTURE LIFE & BUSINESS.

Designing Your Couture Life & Business

"My life didn't please me, so I created my life." – Coco Chanel

You are the designer. You are creating the pattern of your new life. This book is meant to change how you live, love, and treat the world around you. You deserve to design a life you love! Most people never take the time to sit down and do this, whether by circumstance or by choice. Instead they are hustling—always going, working, and staying busy. But they often don't have a true direction or an ideal end result in mind. They are doing what they think they should because someone told them they should, or because they are simply on auto-pilot.

> This is your life, your one and only precious life. It's time for you to take control and design a life you love.

Our goal for this chapter is to sit and reflect in order to visualize the destination of your life and your business. One powers the other, and vice versa. Yes, it's going to take time, and yes, it might be a hard road. Planning your path takes effort but once you know where you're going, life tends to fall into place accordingly. By defining steps that help you work toward your destination, you will no longer waste time on the things that are distracting you from achieving your big goals. In truth, you will have more time to truly *live*—more time with your family and those you love. You'll no longer allow yourself to get caught up in the whirlwind of hustling that goes nowhere. You'll have a destination, defined priorities, and a clear definition of what success means to you.

Before we begin your design process, here's an important note on celebration. Many of us set goals but don't celebrate when we reach them. By the time we finally achieve what we set out to do, we most likely have already set a new goal. This gets tiring—reaching all the time, never stopping to see the progress we have made. The design process that follows was developed so when you set your goals and reach them, you celebrate.

Setting incremental goals lets you celebrate often, making you feel good and eager to do more. Even if things get tough, you have the promise of something good ahead. You focus on the end goal, not the obstacles. Did Gabrielle Bonheur "Coco" Chanel face obstacles in her life? As a woman in business in the world of high fashion, she certainly did. Let's briefly recap the life of Coco: she was born in a poorhouse and lived with her parents and five siblings in one-room. Her mother died when she was twelve and her father sent her to a convent that ran an orphanage—it was here she learned how to sew. Now we can see this may have been a blessing, but making clothing for herself and the other girls in the orphanage probably did not feel like one at the time. At eighteen she moved away from the orphanage and found employment as a seamstress and began singing in the cabaret, where she acquired the stage name "Coco." She wanted to be a singer and auditioned tirelessly, but failed to find stage work. At the age of twenty-three, after much rejection, she realized it was time to change direction. She went back to what she knew—fashion—and opened her first boutique in 1910. At a time when few women ran their own businesses, Chanel flourished, despite obstacles such as war, affairs, scandal, and the threat of many male couture designers. I have to believe this is because of the hardship, the failures, and the foundation she had; she was a fighter who knew what she wanted and how to do it gracefully.

Coco focused on the pattern she was establishing, not the dropped stitches.

Along my path to reaching end goals, I have also faced my fair share of complications. Growing up, I had dyslexia, slow reading comprehension, and a math aversion. These learning disabilities could easily have prevented me from going to college and entering the world of business. Instead, I chose to learn how to work through problems instead of around them. We are going to do the same for you and your business.

We will create a plan for your life, identify potential obstacles, and brainstorm ways through them. This is how we deal with circumstances that are out of our control. It's not the circumstances that dictate our lives, but what we do with them that counts. Do we freeze up and shut down, or do we act? By focusing on what we *can* control, we get a lot further.

Conversely, sometimes decisions arise that you can foresee. You set your path, knowing which obstacles will come up and where you want to stand when they do.

In either scenario, if you know what your end goal is, you can make clear decisions and stick to them. Remember: you are the designer of your life, and you're already planning it out—down to every last, gorgeous detail.

> "I believe that we are solely responsible for our choices, and we have to accept the consequences of every deed, word, and thought throughout our lifetime."
> —Elizabeth Kübler-Ross

I want you to pause for a moment and realize something astounding: *you are completely in control.* In the process I'm about to describe, you are in charge. Throughout this book you will be assessing your values, answering questions, pondering your own life, and beginning to design it.

You will have decisions to make. They are all yours, and yours alone.

Conceptualize | Session #1
current situation

Now it's time we get to work. Are you ready? Throughout these pages you'll come across Conceptualize Sessions: my invitation for you to dive deep and start designing the life and business you love.

So now, grab a pen and your copy of the OWN IT workbook (or your journal, if you don't have the workbook).

Ask yourself: What do you really, truly want? What has been stopping you? How are you going to get there? Jot down whatever comes to mind. Sometimes your first reaction is a reflection of your passion, bubbling to the surface. List broad ideas. Don't dwell on the details yet. We will be diving deeper in each chapter.

That last question is vital. If you have no idea, pause here and give yourself a deadline to figure it out—no longer than a month. Give yourself a chance to deeply reflect and answer this question before moving on.

Now, the next question that we are going to help you answer throughout the course of this book is: *How do you plan to get where you're going?*

One of my dearest friends, Cecelia, has highlighted the value of choices for me. She always reminds me not to panic when I run into a problem—I have control. I get to decide what happens next. She stops me and asks, "What do you want?" In some cases I stubbornly reply, "Well, what I *want* is not an option. These are my choices." She gently reminds me that there is *always* another option, another choice that could help me get to exactly where I want to be, or help the situation turn out the way I want it to. So I think outside the box. What if you were to do the same?

Cecelia is the best example of this "creative choices" mentality in how she lives, too. Cecelia recently had a baby girl. She and her husband agreed to not give their child his last name, nor her maiden name. Instead, they decided to create a new last name for their family. I love the last name they chose: the Sterlings. It sounded so perfect that I went home after a coffee date with Cecelia and told my husband that I wanted to change our last name, too. "Doesn't 'the Goldens' sound *amazing*? The Goldens are definitely good friends of the Sterlings." He laughed, likely a little scared that I actually might try to change our last name. (He knows once I get an idea in my head it's hard to stop me.)

This example perfectly illustrates how you always have a choice. You get to decide. You choose. You choose your path, you choose your business—you can even choose your own last name.

I hope as we work through each chapter, you'll keep in mind that you are in control. Even if you can't influence every variable, you get to decide how you do things. Ideally, you'll take the principles that follow and apply them to your business and your life in new and different ways. You'll learn to separate what is within your power and what is not. Focus only on what you are able to do, and release your focus from the things you can't change. As the Serenity Prayer states, "God, grant me the serenity to accept the things I cannot change, the courage to change the things I can, and the wisdom to know the difference."

Let's be clear: it's you, and only you, who gets to make your own choices. Now it's time to make space in your life to protect the choices you are about to make! That's how you will own them.

Although you may think you have always been in control, it might not actually be the case. You may have made choices in the past out of obligation to someone else: your parents, spouse, children, boss, employee, someone who relied on you, or whom you felt you needed to make proud. At that point, *they* were in charge. You can change that.

Conceptualize | Session #2

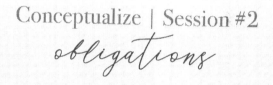

obligations

Grab your OWN IT workbook or your journal and write down some choices you have made out of obligation. What did you do because someone else told you to? What did you do because someone proclaimed it was the right choice? Often, advice, directions, and obligations are assigned to you based on someone else's unique experience and beliefs. Someone else is not you! Stay conscious of this.

You may need to get rid of some obligations you currently have—or think you have—in order to make new, transformative decisions.

Letting go of regrets, fears, and doubts is a crucial step in making space for what's to come. By holding on to negative past experiences or poor choices, you allow them to control your future. To make room in your life for the beautiful things that are to come, you must let go of the past. Past mistakes are just lessons. Thank them, then let them go.

When was the last time you did something because you saw someone else doing it? Your competition, someone else in your industry, or someone you admire? It's okay. We all pay attention to and often copy the actions of others. We look at the way people have done things before, then we try to replicate their process. It's human nature. However, I have learned to choose very carefully whom I emulate.

At age twenty, when starting my first business, Couture Events, I looked to those who had gone before me, those I thought were the best of the best. I set out to know them, to be where they were, to do what they did, in order to learn from them. Smart, right?

There was one woman in the wedding industry whom I really admired. We both were invited to the same conference, and she was asked to share the top current wedding trends and show how she was using them in her events. She shared tips and what she was currently working on with her clients. It was inspiring. As we left, I caught up with her so I could ask her how she got to where she was in the business.

We got in the elevator, just the two of us, and the doors closed. I said to her, "Wow, I love your vision and your creativity. I would love to learn more about how you got to where you are."

I meant it as a compliment, but you'd never guess what happened next. Without warning she turned to me, grabbed my face with both hands, and said, "You'd better not steal any of my ideas!"

First of all, there is never a reason to touch someone else's face (well, unless you are giving them a much needed facial.) I was in disbelief, shaken that she had touched me and spoken so harshly. Second I thought, why was she threatened by me? I was new in the industry and so young. I had only been trying to pay her a compliment.

I realized then she was not who I wanted to become. I could tell she was jaded, burnt out, unsure, and not confident in her own abilities. In trying to mask her insecurity, she showed me her true colors, and they weren't pretty. I set out to make sure I'd be different.

When I started to look at those who had "made it" in my industry, I saw this was a common theme—jealousy, insecurity, pettiness. I set out never to become "her" or "him." I wanted to welcome new people to my industry, to help it thrive. I wanted to lead, and be a light to those around me. As my skills have evolved, I remain confident in what I can offer and secure that no one else can do it the same way I do. The stress my would-be mentor carried around—the burden and suspicion of someone out to "steal her ideas"—were signs of *the opposite of* a purposeful life. And they zapped her power.

This is what I mean when I say to mind your own business and stop worrying about others. Being so afraid of others taking your ideas can be crippling. Just be unique! Be authentic. The only way to shine is to show what you can do, and not worry about what others are doing. Copying other people can be dangerous. It can hold you back. To be confident in yourself and your business, you have to stop looking around and look inside. This doesn't mean you can't admire or be inspired by others, but don't idolize them. There is probably a lot you are not seeing as well; I was lucky to get a glimpse of that woman's shortcomings.

Today, when I speak at events or help other young entrepreneurs, I seek to ask them revealing questions, to truly see them, and to speak vision into their lives. I'm not threatened by their gifts or goodness... because I'm confident in mine.

I'm a huge Disney fan. The live-action films *Maleficent* and *Cinderella* demonstrate in a behind-the-scenes manner why the villains in the Disney classics are the way they are. The bitterness that arises from sorrow, loss, or hardship creates the perfect villain for these fictional stories. But that insight comes from real life. The woman who I admired showed me her villain side. I am sure she has some unpleasant experiences in her past that have made her the way she is. I can't help but be sympathetic, let go of that incident, but still learn from it. This is what I want you to be able to do. I want you to learn from difficulties, but not grow bitter. Dwelling on them is a trap. Villains are just victims who are unable to let go of their past.

Don't let adversity define you. Some measure of it is unavoidable. This is called life, and don't forget: life intersects with business. Ten years of ups and downs have shown me the best thing you can do is mind your own business, and let go of the rest.

> "In order to be irreplaceable,
> one must always be different"
> —Coco Chanel

That unpleasant encounter made it clear: I needed to be different. I needed to set things up in my life and in my business so I would not burn out, feel threatened, or focus on negative events or past frustrations. I set out to be an inspiration and not act out of fear. I would aim to encourage and empower other young entrepreneurs, instead of being intimidated by them or simply trying to be better than them.

It is okay to take what others are doing and learn from it, but don't replicate it. If it's been done, it's been done. I know that may seem silly, but the truth is if someone else has done it and been successful at it, you probably won't get to where they are by doing it the same way. Your time is precious—don't waste it. Refocus your energy on your uniqueness, and start creating the *you* that you want to be.

Danielle Mulvey, an incredible profit guide and great friend, gave me this advice: "I like to be a maverick, and I want you to be a maverick about how you do things. Just because it's been done before doesn't mean it's the best way. You have to do things a little bit differently to get the attention the last thing once got."

So, how do we do this?

Conceptualize | Session #3 & #4
creative concepts for your life & business

This conceptualization is to help you form creative ideas to get your mind moving in a new way. Let's start with any intention you've had in the past but have had a hard time achieving or taking action on. First, come up with three intentions for your life (keep this personal, do not include your business). Second, do this with your business (and do not include anything personal). Now create a list, ranking these intentions (1-6), and start with the intention that would make the greatest impact if it were to become a reality. Let's make a roadmap together for these top six ideas. List out point A (where you are now with this intention) and point B (where you want to get to). Now, make a list of all the ways to get there that you have traditionally seen done before. Then, think outside the box. Redesign the traditional idea. *What else could you do that would be similar to this but NOT exactly the same? Now write down those off the wall ideas and crazy thoughts that you are afraid to put to paper. Could these reap the same result you ultimately want?*

Take each of these ideas and rank them inside of each intention (1...). You should now have six intentions, each with many ranked ideas or ways you could achieve them. Take your best idea and try it out first. Get feedback from family and close friends, use your instagram following, ask for accountability, use your resources. I think it will help you see some of the changes you are hoping to make in your life and business. We are going to dive in so much deeper, this is just a start to get your creative juices flowing and get you thinking in a new way. We'll go further from here.

My husband and I have been doing game nights with friends for the last couple of years and he always wants to tell me how to play. When we were first married, it was cute that he wanted to help me. But, as the years went on, I had to find a way out of this dynamic. I needed to play my own way, and I told him so. He couldn't always recognize when I needed more autonomy.

So, we developed a phrase, *"You do you"*—which means *you* get to decide how you want to play the game, now let me decide how I want to play. You do you, I will do me. It's now a joke amongst our friends and family. When anyone is trying to tell someone else how to do something they'd rather figure out on their own, the response is, "You do you."

This is a great metaphor for all of life: you *have* to do you! You are unique, creative, beautiful, smart, talented. Trust your gut and do what you know is right in your heart.

You might be like me and wish there was just one road to take, one way to do things. I like to do things "the right way." I used to try looking for the one way to do something and would be sadly disappointed when I found out everyone does that thing differently. After ten years I have come to realize in business and in life there are so many paths to success, you have to blaze your own way. If you follow someone else's path, you set yourself up for disappointment. You may also miss out on something truly special and right for you.

As you work on the principles in this book, if you find yourself getting too caught up in what I am asking for, flip the equation. Ask yourself what you can get out of what I'm asking versus feeling like you need to do it a certain way. When I offer guidance, I'm not saying, *My way or the highway.* I'm really saying, *You do you.*

CHAPTER

2

PASSION, PURPOSE & SUCCESS

SUCCESS,
PASSION & PURPOSE

Success

suc·cess | \sək-ˈses \

noun

1: outcome, result
2: a degree or measure of succeeding
     b favorable or desired outcome
also the attainment of wealth, favor, or eminence
: one that succeeds

— Merriam-Webster Dictionary

Ah, the official definition of success. But what does success mean to you? Maybe it means being the ruler of your own world. If so, you'll need to envision what that looks like. When you achieve everything you want, what will you have?

Imagine the very best version of yourself five years from now. Sometimes success brings its own challenges. What does your life look like? If all of your dreams come true: who are you? Where are you? Are you feeling satisfied and whole?

Most people who have reached their goals and achieved what they thought would be "success" find out they still want more. Why is this? Likely because they didn't consider in advance *who* they would be if they were their most successful selves.

History shows us people who define success as being a millionaire may reach their goal at the expense of their family and friends, ending up without love in their life. Others who define success as having love in their lives realize love won't pay the bills—or support their loved ones.

Success is complex. In this chapter, I want you to break it down. You will need to define your own success as it's different for every person. Let's start by defining your purpose.

I know defining your purpose can feel overwhelming, so carve out the space and time you need. Let's start with some important definitions:

> **Success:** the accomplishment of an aim or purpose
>
> **Purpose:** the reason for which something is done or created or for which something exists
>
> **Passion:** a strong feeling of enthusiasm or excitement for something or about doing something

Conceptualize | Session #5

passion

What makes you excited? What brings you great joy and fulfillment? What makes you ready for each new day?

Pull out your OWN IT notebook (or your journal) and list out the things you are passionate about. There's no "perfect" answer here; just let your imagination run.

What you've written down is likely related to your job, your family, and your everyday life. This is good. Now let's take it one step further and ask, Why are you passionate about these things? These are hints toward figuring out your purpose.

When I first did this exercise, years ago, it looked something like this:

- I am an event designer.
- I get excited when I can make something new.
- I love making inspiration boards for our couples so they can see what their wedding day will look like.
- I love curating photo shoots and collaborating with other vendors to make something beautiful.
- I love that I get to help someone by bringing their dreams to reality on their wedding day.
- I love the feeling of accomplishment after helping a brand launch their newest product.
- I love creating experiences for people that they will have as memories for the rest of their lives.

- I have a vision for myself and others and I love to see the vision come to life.

Now, if I were to look back at my life, growing up, here were my passions:

- I loved making animals out of molding clay.
- I always kept a journal; I loved writing down inspirational quotes, cutting clippings out of magazines and making collages, and brainstorming new concepts.
- I loved to decorate my backpack, personalize it, make it unique.
- I loved being the leader. I formed an "animal club" (and immediately made myself the president). Members would visit local animal shelters and work with the dogs and cats.
- I loved leading craft making as a camp counselor.
- I loved being on student council and creating events for my classmates.
- During my freshman year of college, I designed my own clothing line.
- During my junior year of college, I started my own business.

I took time to evaluate: what elements of these passions brought me joy or happiness? In looking at each of these points, I was able to find a common thread I hadn't seen before—an enduring enjoyment in what I could do. I saw that my purpose is to *create and inspire.*

So, no matter what my current passion is (and interests do change), I am able to live in my purpose and find fulfillment. That is the difference between your *purpose*, which will remain the same in all stages of life, and your *passion*, which will change and grow with you.

In whatever I do now or in the future, whether it's writing this book, speaking to entrepreneurs, leading a circus, or even flying to the moon, I know that if I am *creating and inspiring*, I will be living my purpose and I will be fulfilled.

I once spoke to a group of photographers, and I asked them to complete this exercise. One photographer, Erica Schnider shared:

> *"I love to give direction to my clients to make them look their very best. I love photographing families and children. I love raising my kids. I love cooking organically and taking care of my family. I love helping other photographers and mentoring them in their business. The common thread I just discovered is "nurture." My purpose is to nurture."*

I was invited to speak about passion and purpose at a University and after I was done one of the professors told me she realized after doing the exercise and listing out her passions that her purpose is to *"gain knowledge"* in order to share it with those who need it. She spends time informing herself, collecting information, and learning so she can help others understand and learn. It's important to get at what lies beneath your passions, to reveal what motivates you.

Sometimes, identifying your purpose can alter your direction completely. This next story about purpose really hit home. Stephanie was a pharmacist who loved her job, but found the long hours to be draining and her work becoming stale. As a hobby, she loved taking photos. She never thought she could make a job out of it; she just loved taking meaningful photos at friends' weddings, family sessions, and birthday parties.

One day, one of her friends called and asked if she still had newborn photos of their daughter, whom she learned had sadly passed away from cancer. "Of course I do," she responded.

The mother called later in tears. At first, Stephanie thought maybe she had made things harder by sharing the pictures. A few minutes passed and the mom blurted out, "Your photos are healing. These photographs are helping me heal." In that moment, Stephanie understood that both as a pharmacist and as a photographer, the thing that made her feel the most alive was the act of healing others.

Living your purpose isn't always obvious or traditional. Stephanie wasn't a nurse or a doctor, but she was healing with her gifts, which brought her fulfillment. She wound up leaving the pharmacy to become a full time photographer. She now photographs women who have lost their self-confidence after having breast cancer, in order to help them see themselves in a new way and begin the process of healing.

Each of us want to do good in the world, and we will each do it in different ways. We have been created with a purpose to bring to the table. When you consciously identify what your purpose is, you can better *share it* with others. Bam! Success. So, figuring out your overriding purpose first will help you define your unique interpretation of success.

> "When you are living in your purpose and you are defining your own success, this is when you have made it!"
> - Krystel Stacey

Yes, I just quoted myself. Why? Because I believe so strongly in this philosophy. You must first define your purpose and your idea of success before they can become a realization.

Conceptualize | Session #6

purpose

Do you know what your purpose is? Some of us have one main purpose and some have a few competing ones. Note: you probably don't have more than three. Start by naming your current passions and then look back at the past. When looking for purpose, rule out things that are innately in all of us, like helping people, loving others, and the longing for legacy. Look at not just these things but the deeper why or how. How will you help others, and why do you want to love others?

Okay, now we are going to start digging *really* deep. Tell me: what is the purpose of your life? Why are you here on this earth? I recognize this is a question you've been trying to answer since high school, or even before then, but I want you to sit and think about it—again— with intention.

I asked this to a group of creative entrepreneurs, and one of the outspoken creatives in the group (who also happens to be an attorney) responded, "This is a question I have been struggling with my whole f***ing life, and you want me to answer it in an hour during this workshop?" My answer to this: *Yes,* because I know you can. I know it's there, it always has been, you just need to figure it out and then declare it to yourself and the world every day.

Everyone has a purpose in life, a reason for living, a reason for caring. It's that "something" that makes you who you are. At your core, it is your purpose. Your purpose *does not* change. It will remain the same throughout your entire life. Once you identify your purpose, you can apply it to many different passions. Passions will evolve, ebbing and flowing like the tide as you grow and mature.

Some people go through life never knowing or articulating their purpose. They feel it's too big a question. They are scared to even ask themselves what their purpose is. They worry, *"What if I can't find it?"* Guess what: it's still there. Whether we consciously think about it or not, we *all* have a purpose. So, why not define it? "Minding your own business" is the process of getting to know yourself a bit better, to fully understand your own purpose, so that you can *own* your life and your business. That's the first step toward success. Go ahead; put your purpose into words. And take your time.

List these all out. Now, out of the three to five things you are left with, what stands out to you? What makes you feel *the most fulfilled?* It will almost seem so obvious you'll wonder how you ever missed it. That's your purpose.

As Brendon Burchard, author of *High Performance Habits* puts it, you know you were successful if you were to look back at the end of your life and you can answer "yes" to the following questions:

Did I live?
Did I love?
Did I matter?

How beautiful and oh, how true. We all want to *live* and feel *alive* every day. We all want to love deeply and be loved and known in return. We all want to make an impact; to leave a legacy and make our lives matter. So, the question is *how* are you going to do it? Be specific. Narrow it down so you can reach it. Make sure when you do, you will feel satisfied, and it will truly feel like success.

We are going to evaluate your life, dig deeper, and dream bigger than ever before. When I think about my most successful self, it becomes more clear when I write it down. I discover things that spell out *success* for me. I want you to do the same.

To me, success is (in no particular order):

- Sleeping in and waking up when I want to (I am not a morning person as you will learn in chapter five. Timing does have a major impact on my productivity.)

- Running my own schedule, rather than conforming to someone else's

- Being my own boss

- Being in the business of joy, using my purpose

- Creating experiences and beautiful things, and inspiring others

- Having an incredible team I get to lead (I love working with and mentoring other people)

- Being able to spend time with my family (this is huge)

- Hearing God saying: "Well done, my good and faithful servant." (I know I've used the talents He gave me to grow and better the kingdom)

For me, the money itself is not the goal, but being able to buy that latte or salted caramel ice cream any dang time I want to? Yes! *That's success!*

If money is your idea of success, I'd like you to think about why that is. What's the root of it for you? What will the money get you? There is probably a connection there, a deeper reason why money is correlated with success in your mind.

The way we think about money is formed by the way we were raised. Growing up, I watched those around me make a lot of money—and lose a lot of money. Money is something I have seen people go crazy over. But it also comes and goes. To me, cash has nothing to do with happiness, because I have seen those who have no money be very happy and those who are wealthy be very lost and miserable. To me, money is pieces of paper and metal! That's it! It's something I can trade in to get the things I need or want, but it is *not* security or happiness. It is nice to be able to take a friend out to dinner, give away ten percent of revenue to a nonprofit, or do something else positive with surplus funds. Don't get me wrong: I am not opposed to money being a part of success for you. Just make sure you look at why it is.

To some of you, money may mean security. To others, acres of land you can call your own might mean success. Or, perhaps, being able to cook a meal for your family every night might be part of your success. Don't let someone else tell you what it is. *You do you,* remember? Define what success is for you. Break it down line by line (like I do above), and then we will put it all together. At the end of this chapter, you are going to sum it up and define success for yourself.

Conceptualize | Session #7
define success

Write out what the most *successful* version of you is doing in five years. What does your life look like? What does your day-to-day look like? Where do you live? Who are you spending time with? Who are your friends? What do you do for fun? What do you do for work?

Remember to "mind your own business." Instead of looking at what others have done and how they have done it, try to think outside of the box and dream *big*. It's okay to have thoughts that don't line up with your current reality. There will be time later on to make an action plan.

> Seriously, for now—keep your head in the clouds.
> Dream, girl, dream! Write it all down.

Once we define what "successful you" looks like, we can break down what *makes* you successful and reverse engineer it to get you there. Don't worry about who will see these dreams. It's like making a wish before blowing out the candles. That wish is for you to know. The *how* isn't important right now; just the *what* and the *why.* These will give you the right idea of what "successful you" looks like.

Remember the Conceptualize Sessions #3 & #4—point A to point B brainstorm—we did together in Chapter One? Let's revisit; this time, in terms of your path to success.

Conceptualize | Session #8
path to success

What does Successful You have that you currently don't?

How are you going to get it?

What do you need to get to this point?

How would the most successful version of you describe success?

Conceptualize | Session #9
the future

Now, write out what Successful You looks like, as if she already exists. Here is my example:

> *I wake up grateful and full of intention. I know what my goals are for the day. I have a beautiful plan, but I am flexible in knowing things will not always go my way. I can wake up and go for a walk or go to coffee with a friend or my mom (relationships are important to me and I don't have a nine-to-five job). I get to be at home with my baby three days a week, and I get to go to work two days a week, which is a blessing. I live in a sweet little home in my favorite small neighborhood—full of love and grace. I have a husband who is crazy*

in love with me and I am madly in love with him. We have a daughter whom we spend time with and we get to teach her about the beauty of life. She is able to do all of the things she wants to do (we are able to provide for her). She has ambition (and understands hard work will get her to where she wants to be), and she has big dreams for herself. We travel at least once a month and see the world together. We celebrate life with special experiences instead of "stuff." I get to go on adventures for work, taking my speaking, creating, and inspiring with me. I get to make dreams come true for brides with our wedding coordination company, create magical moments for people with our lifestyle events company, and I help entrepreneurs focus and "mind their own business." I spread light and love wherever I go.

I want to enjoy my life. Be able to work only a few hours a day and not feel guilty about it (like I should be hustling more). I want to create, inspire, and have a happy family and home life. I say this not to provoke envy or define your success, but to show you what inspires me to reach for success.

What would make you beyond eager to wake up every day? What would make your heart flutter with excitement? What would make you say, "I can't believe this is my life!"

Write it down.

All of the things you list are important. Next, isolate the pieces that are *most* important to you to define success on your terms.

> I will make everything around me beautiful,
> that will be my life.
> —Elsie de Wolf

Here is my definition of success, based on my purpose that motivates me:

> I will **inspire** those around me to become better. To remember who they were before others broke them down. Reminding myself and them daily to be the people they were made to be. Bringing vision and providing clarity. I will create every day and dream big. I will live out the life I have imagined. I will bring joy to those around me and be a light to those who know me. I will live a life of purpose, not just a life of what comes my way.

If I do all of the above, my life will have been successful. That's what it means to me. Don't let society define success for you if it doesn't match up with what you want. Decide what makes you happy. That doesn't mean you can't learn from other people. Here is how some others have defined success:

- "Too many people measure how successful they are by how much money they make or the people that they associate with. In my opinion, true success should be measured by how **happy** you are." —billionaire Richard Branson

- "To live the lives we truly want and deserve, and not just the lives we settle for, we need a Third Metric, a third measure of success that goes beyond the two metrics of money and power, and consists of four pillars: **well-being, wisdom, wonder, and giving**." —*Huffington Post* co-founder Arianna Huffington

- "I measure success by **how many people love me**." — legendary investor Warren Buffet

- "Success is **liking yourself, liking what you do**, and **liking how you do it**." — poet Maya Angelou

- "If you carefully consider **what you want to be said of you in the funeral experience**, you will find *your* definition of success." —author Stephen Covey

There's nothing wrong with sharing a purpose with others, or considering what drives them as a template for what you might accomplish. But don't stop there.

Remember: "*You do you!*"

3.

VALUES

AND

PRIORITIES

VALUES & PRIORITIES

Time, money, family, work, health, wealth, love, happiness. These are some of the top values I've found speaking to women I've worked with over the past ten years. Perhaps many of these apply to you as well.

Values give us our drive, and when we lose that drive we stop believing in our own worth. That's when negative thoughts start to creep into our lives. A value system is made up of checks and balances. When you're down for the count in one area of value, you realize how much you treasure it because you fall out of alignment. Values are a deeply ingrained part of who we are.

A life and business you love calls for balance in our values. There are core values, which are shared by many, and there are personal values, which are more specific to each individual. You cherish your personal values because they reflect what you've learned from your life experience. These may be formed due to your upbringing, your faith, your family, your lessons learned, or even things you don't have but wish you did.

Let's start with a look at the values by which you live, big and small.

Conceptualize | Session #10
core values

Write down everything you value. What values do you hold above all else? These may be things like fairness, respect for others, and other general human values.

Now, think about your personal convictions. What tugs on your heartstrings that may be unique to you? These may be your personal interests, such as being a reliable friend or helping people who are less fortunate. These are your personal values. They are beautiful, and they are a part of what makes you, you. Cherish these. Don't forget about them—they will play into so much of your success and your goal setting.

Now that you have written out your values, we are going to focus on your priorities. We can't do or care about everything with equal attention. How you prioritize your concerns and actions will affect how you put yourself out into the world.

> There are twelve pillars of your life that I believe are the keys to happiness.

These have been compiled from motivational speakers such as Chalene Johnson, Tony Robbins, along with the organization,

Action for Happiness. Everyone is in a different place with how they feel about each one, and other people may look at your life and think something different. The truth is inside of you and you need to decide for yourself where you rank in each area.

Don't spend too long on this next exercise. Go with your gut, assigning priority by the first number that comes to mind. These twelve areas of your life represent your unique realm of "happiness" or, as the French say, your *joie de vivre* (joy of living). These areas are highly valued and must be balanced and in good shape before you can focus your energy elsewhere. Mind your own business! Focus inward. It's okay to be vulnerable.

Conceptualize | Session #11

Twelve key areas of joie de vivre

STEP 1: A DEEP DIVE

Rate your level of fulfillment with each area of your life below. Use a scale of 1 to 10, with 1 being *extremely dissatisfied/very unfulfilled* and 10 being *extremely satisfied and fulfilled*. Each area will be rated individually, meaning each could end up with the same rating. I include descriptive examples for each section, but remember fulfillment and happiness should be defined solely by you.

1. **Surroundings.** This is where you spend most of your day and includes the following: your environment, the town you live in, your home, your garden, the office, your living space, your car, your bedroom, and even your closet. Your environment is influenced by those you live with so consider them a part of it. How much joy do your surroundings bring you?

   Rating: _____

2. **Recreation & Relaxation.** This is the fun stuff: your vacation time, free time, hobbies, fun pursuits outside of work like movies, sports, reading, journaling, painting, leisurely walks, and activities you use to recharge. Consider the frequency and quality of your recreation/relaxation time. How satisfied with it are you?

   Rating: _____

3. **Personal Growth.** This area encompasses your efforts to be a better you. It includes developmental activities like attending conferences, seminars, workshops, self-improvement reading, and educational pursuits. It also covers less formal attempts at growth: introspective reflection, bettering your interpersonal skills, reading this book ;) and anything you do to improve habits and skills. You may do these things subconsciously to advance self-awareness and iden-

tity or enhance the quality of your life. Or they may be intentional—meant to develop specific talents, to increase your employability, or to realize dreams and aspirations. How is this working out for you?

Rating: _____

4. **Spirituality & Faith.** This area includes your belief in a higher power, God, or a metaphysical force greater than the physical world. This area can include your devotion to your religion, divinity, faith, or the practice of honoring powers that transcend the physical world. Also consider prayer, devotion, meditation and/or the practice of being "present," living in the moment. How much personal satisfaction do you gain from your practices—or lack of them?

    Rating: _____

5. **Purpose & Career.** This includes your profession, volunteer work, following your passion, and doing what you believe you've been called to do. It also includes knowing and understanding your *why*. Do you use your talents or any work/knowledge/training/skill/or natural ability in a way that has a positive effect on others? Do you believe who you are, what you do, and how you use your "calling" and gifts positively affects others?

    Rating: _____

6. **Finances.** This includes your relationship with money: your current savings, lack of debt, sound investments, and financial independence. Related issues, like your understanding of your financial situation, your ability to afford the things you want, and the outlook for your financial future also contribute to your state of mind. How satisfied are you with these things?

   Rating: _____

7. **Friends & Family Relationships.** This area includes your parents, siblings, and close relationships you might have with extended family members. It also includes your relationship with a small circle of close friends. Put together, how fulfilling do you find the level of mutual support, respect, "real" communication, and your personal and emotional connections with friends and family?

   Rating: _____

8. **Romantic Relationship(s).** This area can include your significant other, your dating relationships, and/or your spouse. This is a measure of your emotional and physical connection with a romantic

partner. In evaluating this area, take into consideration your mutual support, respect, appreciation and friendship. Take into account shared hobbies, quantity and quality of time spent together, and your physical and intimate connection. How well do you feel supported by and connected to your partner(s)?

Rating: _____

9. **Fitness & Physical Health.** This is a broad category but generally includes your overall "wellness." Think about the factors of your physical health: regular diet, stress management, sleep, exercise, and nutrition. What degree of flexibility, strength, and energy do they result in? Are you satisfied with your weight? Does your level of fitness—and the things you do to achieve it—make you happy?

Rating: _____

10. **Emotional Health.** This category includes how you feel about yourself and your importance to others. How easily do you feel and express (when appropriate) a wide range of emotions without feeling unsafe or insecure? Mental wellness includes your overall happiness, a feeling of being whole, satisfied and at peace with your past. Mental wellness is your ability to handle stress and life's unexpected turns.

How often do you feel sad, angry, depressed, shame, or emptiness. How "okay" are you with yourself?

Rating: _____

11. **Giving.** This area is about how you are contributing to the world around you. Are you giving back in various ways that you are able to with your time, talents, knowledge, and finances? Is there more you could be doing to give to your family, tribe, community or the greater good? Think about your God given gifts and how you can use them to serve. How do you feel about what you are offering in each of these areas?

Rating: _____

12. **Explore.** This category is about how often you are willing to get out of your comfort zone. This could be in trying new things, exploring new areas, delving into new endeavors, and your sense of adventure. Are you feeling complacent or fulfilled in this area?

Rating: _____

Great things never came from comfort zones.

STEP 2: A SHIFT IN FOCUS

Congrats, you did it! You just compiled your answers with intention to create a diamond in the rough. Now review your answers from Step 1. Put a check mark next to any area that you rated a 6 or below, and a star next to any area that received a score of 7 or higher.

Go over those stars. Those areas in which you rated 7 or higher—amazing! Take a moment to feel incredible about these aspects of your life. You are really doing well here! Write these down, and find a way to celebrate each one. Reward yourself for your hard work in whatever way you see fit, and keep it up.

Look over those check marks—those you rated 6 or below. These areas of lower satisfaction actually present great opportunities. Take some time to think about why you rated yourself low in these categories. Often, these are areas in which your interest or concern is growing, or in which you want to improve, but are having a hard time figuring out where to start.

Now ask yourself *why?* What's holding you back? What are three things you *could* do to improve these areas?

You can dig deep here, in your *OWN IT* workbook, or in your personal journal. Many times, we rate ourselves low in areas of less concern to us. Why aren't these things more important? Maybe because they are foreign to you, or because you just don't have enough information about them.

For example, for me finance has consistently ranked low. Why? Perhaps because I knew I hated numbers, so I told myself I didn't have a desire to learn. The truth is, deep down, financial subjects scared me. I thought I wouldn't understand them, and if I did, would I even *want* to know?

Sometimes, you have to put your brave face on and own your fears. Of course I want to know. I need to know about how to manage my money. No one else will do it for me. Instead of getting defensive about your low-ranking areas of satisfaction, get practical about them. If they're important to your livelihood or well-being, like your finances or health, step up to the plate. If they're related to your recreational life, the priority will clearly be lower.

Now is the time to work on the area(s) you ranked low, one at a time. These are the keys to your happiness. You can start with the most pressing topic, or work your way up via easier ones. Resist the urge to work on everything at once. Start with just one area and make it your key priority for the next period of your life. Maybe it's one month, six months, or a year, but set a date and focus on meeting your goal.

RESULTS: CORE PRIORITIES VS. KEY PRIORITIES

Now that you've reviewed those ten areas of your life, let's talk about setting priorities that will further your quest for happiness and fulfillment. I first learned about the different types of priorities from health and lifestyle expert Chalene Johnson. As she puts it: Core priorities are things that you value continually, but key priorities require your focus immediately. She is also the pillar to my goal-setting foundation as she taught me how to create goals and a system that I am now going to share with you in the next chapter, with my own twist.

I know many women who believe if they value something, it should always remain a key priority, requiring their constant vigilance. Not the case. In fact, if you already have a habit of doing something well, then you no longer need to make it a priority (although you do certainly need to keep doing it).

For example, my work is a priority in my life. I have been working for eight-plus hours every weekday for the last ten years. I love my work. I love the feeling of accomplishment and checking things off my work to-do list. This is obviously something I value but no longer needs to be a priority, as I have already made a habit out of it. Because work is easily integrated into my life, I don't need to put as much thought, energy, and effort into it. I should still spend time on my work, but I can start to *prioritize* other pursuits that aren't automatic habits yet. When we talk about key priorities, they should be things you *need* to focus on right now.

Here are the tools that will provide the keys to your happiness:

Core Priorities vs. Key Priorities

Core Priorities. You don't have to reach for these; they are intrinsic to who you are, the way work is for me. Work is ingrained in me. I like to work, I love to create, no one has to twist my arm. You probably scored high in areas that encompass your core priorities. These are things that already make you happy.

Key Priorities. These shift with the changes in your life. Doing what is most important at the right time is a powerful tool. These priorities are called *key* because they are going to unlock your happiness.

Key priorities change, for instance, when you hit a life milestone. You graduate, get married, retire, lose someone close to you, change careers, have a baby, get in financial trouble, divorce, meet someone new. These defining moments will alter the urgency of what you need to think about or do in your immediate future. Because of this, it's good to sit down and reevaluate your key priority every three to six months, or with major milestones in your life.

When I was eight years old, I told my mom I knew exactly what I wanted in life, that I had it all planned out. She said,

> "Oh, darling, your priorities will change."

I remember asking her if it was similar to how I felt about Disneyland rides. She asked what I meant by that. I said, "Well, when I was little, I loved the Dumbo ride. But now, I really love the teacups." She nodded and said, "Yes, honey, it's just like that."

I'm telling you now, your priorities will change, just like my affection for the Dumbo ride! You're growing. You will soon like the teacups, then move on to Splash Mountain, and someday you might prefer Space Mountain. Then, when you have kids of your own, your priorities will change again and you will be back on the Dumbo ride, happy to be there.

It's okay to have your priorities change. It's human, and healthy, and good for your soul. Think of priority shifts as seasons of life. Have you ever had a hard time making a decision in the past because you weren't sure what would be best, or how it would fit into your schedule? You have probably been thinking too much about the long run with your priorities, if that is the case. They don't have to be forever. What we need to focus on is *this* week or *this* month—*right now*, wherever you are at. Figuring out your current key priority will help you make every decision in *this* season of your life. And you'll learn something to apply to the next.

So, look over your scores and brainstorm: what's your key priority? You'll come up with an answer quickly, because you now know what success looks like to you. Only you know what you need to be doing *right now,* in this season, to get there.

Conceptualize | Session #12
key priority

The sense of urgency that informs your key priority comes from a need for accountability in some area of your life. It's what you *need* to change to bring your life back into balance. For me, at one point, it was my finances. I couldn't just wish them away. I had to work at getting them in order.

So, what's your weak spot? Look at those low scores. Among them is your current key priority. Write it down in your *OWN IT* workbook or in your private journal. It's worth it! You know if you spend time focusing on this one thing, everything else in your life will get just a bit better, a little bit sweeter. Acknowledge that.

Now, what are you going to do about it? Write down how you will keep yourself accountable to this key priority. Dive deeper into your workbook. Write down the steps you are going to take in order to keep this key priority your focus at this time in your life.

Conceptualize | Session #13
sweet sixteen key business areas

You've just taken a major step. Now you're ready to follow the same process for your business. What season is it in your professional life? Are you having fun yet? I have identified sixteen areas of business operations that are the *joie de vivre* to a healthy enterprise. I like to consider these the **"sweet sixteen."** I want you to rank your business in each area, on a scale of 1 to 10:

1 = I am *really lacking* this in my business.
10 = I am *incredible* at this!

AREA OF BUSINESS

1. **Branding**: This includes the entire aesthetic of your brand: logo, colors, style, typography, etc.

Rating: _____

2. **Prices and Packaging**: This includes your current packages (services offered or actual physical packaging) and pricing of your services or product.

Rating: _____

3. **Profitability**: How much profit are you keeping? How profitable is your business financially? Are your expenses as lean as they can/should be? Are you paying yourself regularly? Do you have cash on hand or are you operating check to check?

Rating: _____

4. **Processes & Systems**: Have you created standard operating procedures for your company? Do you have step by step processes and systems in place that are clearly defined?

Rating: _____

5. **Team Building**: How are you growing your internal team—not just in size, but in loyalty and education? How are you hiring? How are you firing? Are you delegating properly?

Rating: _____

6. **Marketing**: This includes press, public relations, editorials, and the visibility of your business to the public.

Rating: _____

7. **Environment**: Where do you work? This could be your home office, a public office, or a warehouse. Is the environment around you enabling you to do your job better, be creative, or focus when needed?

Rating: _____

8. **Equipment**: Do you have the equipment you need to run your business properly? Is it updated to current standards?

Rating: _____

9. **Customer Acquisition**: How are you getting your customers ? Do you feel good about the systems you have in place for obtaining new customers?

Rating: _____

10. **Customer Relationship Management (CRM)**: How are you keeping track of the clients you have or have had? How are you managing what needs to be done for them or what has been done for them in the past?

Rating: _____

11. **Customer Service**: What is the customer's experience with your company? Once you have the customers, how effectively are

you communicating with them? And how are they experiencing your brand?

Rating: _____

12. **Networking**: This includes how you are interacting with others to develop contacts and keep up current business relationships. This could include going to events, making a point to meet with new people, and maintaining the contacts you currently have.

Rating: _____

13. **Website**: How do you feel about your current website? Does it match the brand you have created? How is the customer experience on the website? Is your messaging on the site clear?

Rating: _____

14. **Social Media**: This includes your Instagram, Facebook, LinkedIn accounts, and any other social media presence you have. Are you communicating effectively which services you have to offer and creating a cohesive brand with all of your social media? Also, think about your activity on social media.

Rating: _____

15. **Finances & Bookkeeping**: How are you keeping track of your finances? Do you have an effective system for bookkeeping, and are you producing profit and loss statements regularly? Are you reconciling your accounts monthly?

Rating: _____

16. **Leadership & Accountability**: Are you able to lead effectively in your business? Do you have an accountability metric to make sure you are maintaining standards?

Rating: _____

The same is true of business as it is of life: as your business grows, your way of doing things will also change. That's okay! Your operations *should* change. Your business evolves with you and becomes more sophisticated as you grow. It's something you can't plan for. Your tastes and tendencies will vary—with the times, with maturity, and when you pinpoint what matters most to your business right now.

In my fifth year of owning Couture Events, I was afraid of growth or changing our systems because I felt like we should be working the way we always had. I wanted to offer new services, update the current packages, and create a better customer experience—but I was nervous that former clients would find out and demand, "Why weren't we offered this stuff?" I didn't want anyone to feel they had missed out.

It took time for me to realize folks would understand businesses grow, people grow, and things change. If it were for the better, then they would be rooting me on. Honestly, they probably wouldn't notice at all—and in any case, it was my call to make.

Once I realized this, it freed me to grow.

This was no longer the Dumbo ride, my friends.

We were moving on to Splash Mountain, and in another five years, when my business was a "big girl," we'd tackle Space Mountain! Roll with the changes. Find a better way to do things. Don't look back. That's what it's all about.

Stagnant businesses rot. Evolving in your business is a must. What has worked in the past might not work now.

This is part of why I love Instagram history (and haven't deleted any of it). You can see where you started and how far you have come. If your Instagram account looks the same as it did when you started your business five years ago, it's a good indication you are not growing.

Conceptualize | Session #14
key business priority

So, let's set your key business priority to align with where you are right now. The future is always changing, but we have to plan for our reality today. If you were to grow in one area of your business, which would it be? Which main area could you create growth in to open doors to many other possibilities? How are you going to be held accountable for this?

When I first started my wedding coordination business I was still working in "Corporate America." I was just on the edge of jumping into full-time entrepreneurship, and my biggest goal was for one of my weddings to be featured on the largest wedding blog at the time, *Style Me Pretty*. When it finally happened, I was in my office. As soon as I got the email acceptance, I did a little dance in my office and called my mom on my lunch break. I was over-the-moon excited. Little did I know, in the future, our weddings would be featured in print in *The Knot* and *Brides*, and we would actually meet Randy Fenoli from *Say Yes to the Dress*, Hailey Paige—lead designer for JLM Couture, *Harper's Bazaar* weddings and fashion editor Carrie Goldberg, as well as Martha Stewart. I didn't know we would end up attending bridal fashion week in New York, visiting the *Vogue* offices, or planning château weddings in France. I had no idea we would work with *The Real Housewives*, contestants from ABC's *The Bachelor*, or the CEO of an NFL team. We've hosted celebrities at our weddings and have clinked glasses with the best of the best.

Do you see my point? We have come such a long way from that first feature in the wedding blog. But in order to get there, I had to start with a single main priority. My key business priority in marketing eventually turned into one set goal: get featured in a major wedding blog... which turned into so much more.

I look back now and see I had no idea what was in store. My priorities have continued to change, and our business has grown. I have been able to celebrate each victory as I walked along a clear path.

> Of course the unexpected happened, and it wasn't just a straight line to success. But I planned for where I wanted to go. And that's how I got to where I am.

CHAPTER

four

_____

GOAL SETTING

GOAL SETTING

"She believed she could, so she did." While I love this quote so much and I believe you can do anything, I also think you must create a plan, or a "pattern," to get you there and help you reach your goals.

Why is it so hard to accomplish goals? We are so easily distracted by the whirlwind of everyday tasks, we often struggle to focus on one main goal.

Here are the top four reasons we struggle to accomplish goals, according to Dane Sanders, my former business coach:

1. Lack of clarity about our goal

2. Lack of commitment or collaboration to solving the problem

3. Lack of accountability—rarely are we held accountable to meet personal goals

4. Lack of specific action planned or taken to accomplish the goal

Just as a fish discovers water last (or possibly never realizes that it's wet), we often can't see what needs to be done or where we are because we are deep in it. The fundamental obstacle to goal execution is that the whirlwind of day-to-day life keeps us from focusing on any one thing. Life is crazy busy; it's difficult to execute new projects and reach goals when you're just trying to stay above water.

So what do we do? Take time out of that daily whirlwind. Remember to make time to step out on your own, wander off, daydream, think. And do this on a sustained, intentional level periodically, to get those *aha!* moments, like the one that prompted me to write this book.

Jack Johnson wrote a song that resonates with me. I play Jack on repeat at home sometimes but this song, "Wasting Time," really stands out because of the lyrics:

> *"Oh, but everybody thinks*
> *That everybody knows*
> *About everybody else*
> *Nobody knows*
> *Anything about themselves*
> *Cause they're all worried about everybody else."*

———————

We make a point in our culture to always help others. At our best, we are compassionate and selfless. At our worst, we are insecure, abandoning our own wishes and goals. When we desire to know what other people are doing and how they are doing it, we are all up in their business. But this keeps you from realizing your own truths, which may be buried beneath the daily minutiae.

This isn't you anymore. You've started minding your own business, and now you are ready to set your goals and focus on achieving them. The first step is to select goals that will lead to the *results* you want. I call them GEM goals. I love a good gem. My mom was a gemologist, and growing up I loved to look through her collection and pick out my favorites.

> A good goal truly is a gem, something so precious and special you should treasure it!

GEM goals have the following attributes:

G | Gritty—they're very specific and detailed.

E | Effective—the results will make a difference in your life; they're attainable and relevant.

M | Measurable—you're able to measure them and hold yourself accountable with a time frame and a due date.

GEM goals are high in value. They are structured as a template for action and achievement: they are well defined, will produce desired results, and you'll know when you have accomplished them.

These goals you are about to set need to be things you can accomplish in the next ninety days.

Not the full year? *Nope!* Ninety days! Otherwise, you'll lose sight of their urgency and find something else to fill your time.

So, think about it. What can you do in ninety days? Your goals need to be a little bit scary. Don't put things on your list that are going to happen anyway ("I want to walk the dog every day"). Select ambitious goals you almost don't want to show anyone because you are nervous you might not be able to accomplish them. Maybe your friends (or naysayers) would critique you, saying, "Yeah right. You are going to do *that* in the next three months?" So, without having to go through that, you can prove them wrong!

> Your GEM goals set you up for success.

Conceptualize | Session #15
nine gems

The first goal (goal 1) you write down should be about your KEY PRIORITY: a goal that will help you focus on this new area you need to improve upon. Your next two goals (goals 2 & 3) have to do with the next two value areas in your **life** you ranked yourself lowest in, in Chapter 3. Now I want you to write down three goals (goals 4-6) having to do with the three areas you ranked your **business** lowest in. Flip back to Chapter 3 and write one GEM goal for each.

Next, you're going to set three more goals (goals 7-9). You can choose whether it's in business or in your personal life, or a combination of both. These will keep you moving forward and creating a chance to celebrate your progress.

Write them down, either in your *OWN IT* workbook or your own notebook:

- Goal #1 is related to your lowest-ranking value area of your **life** or your key priority

- Goals #2-3 are related to the next two lowest-ranking value areas of your **life**

- Goals #4-6 are related to your three lowest-ranking value areas of your **business and** your new business priorities

- Goals #7-9 are entirely up to you (life or business)

    *To recap, you now have nine goals in total to achieve in the next ninety days that will get you closer to where you want to be.

Now that you have your nine goals for ninety days, write them out as if you are already on the path to achieving them. Write it out for each goal.

I AM _____.
    (Who will you be if you accomplish this goal?)

I HAVE _____.
        (What will you have?)

I DO_____.
    (And what do you now do differently?)

Envision them. Make them real. Can you *see* success?

Are you happy with your nine GEM goals? If, after imagining yourself doing these things and being that person, you really feel these are the best nine goals you've ever set, keep them. If not, really think about whether there is anything that would serve as a better goal for you. Maybe there is an end goal in a different area of your life that would help you get to where you want to be more quickly?

Conceptualize | Session #16
resources

Once you're satisfied each goal is truly going to work toward your best self, take each GEM goal and:

- ☐ Write up to three tasks required to reach each one.

- ☐ Write out the resources you need to complete these tasks. These could be accountability, time, finances, and/ or actual tools or items you need to accomplish each goal.

- ☐ Write out who could help you with this task. Maybe you need to ask someone you know for help or for resources?

Do you notice any resources you wrote down that are repetitive? Is there anything you need that you listed for two or more of your goals? If so, this might help you with your final goal. If not, determine which resources you need the *most* right now.

Okay, final step: you are now going to create a tenth goal that makes most of these other goals possible. We are going to call this your

BRILLIANT goal, because it sheds light on all the other goals. It is the major goal that will help you meet your key priority and accomplish many of your lesser goals.

For example, if I list the resource of "time" next to two or more of my GEM goals, I need to decide how I can make more time in my life. I'll brainstorm all of the things I can do to free up my time:

1.   Cut out TV.

2.   Cut down on other screen time and social media.

3.   Schedule out my time—and stick to it.

4.   Wake up an hour earlier.

I list each idea and then decide what the most effective tactic will be. Maybe cutting out social media and sticking to a schedule is my brilliant goal.

Remember, this is for you to focus on for the next ninety days. Can you do it for that long? *Yes!* Of course, you can. You'll be motivated to get your time back, so you can do the other things you need to do. After ninety days, you'll evaluate if you are going to continue as is, or return to the way things were before. I am sure after that length of time, you will have formed a new habit and filled your free time productively. You may even wonder how you spent so much time on social media in the first place.

Let's say I needed finances to help me with my goals. What could I do *just for the next ninety days* that would help me bring in cash? Let's brainstorm:

1. Work a side job (as a Starbucks barista, a salesperson for Anthropologie, an Uber driver, etc.). How much would that potentially bring in?

2. Offer a sale on my product or service for a limited time to create an urgency to buy from me.

3. Offer a new product or service I'm confident will sell. Maybe this isn't the main focus for the business for the next ninety days; maybe I do this in order to bring in the money needed to fund my other goals.

4. Work at my corporate job for another few months. Yes, I'm ready to quit, but maybe I stay on—or subcontract—to bring in extra revenue.

Your brilliant goal might not be your most important goal or what is most needed in your company or business. But **it's the goal you create to bring you the resources you need the most.** Ultimately, it will get you to where you need to be. You may have to take great risks in accomplishing your brilliant goal. Without a doubt, you'll need to think outside of the box. Again, it will be worth it. Remember my friend Cecelia's advice:

> A solution always exists.

Keep brainstorming. If it's important to you, you will find a way.

Meanwhile, try to not get frozen by the fear of perfection. All you can do is set your goal and see how it goes; this is a starting point. *This can only come from you.* As much as you want to ask someone else what they think, or to confirm that you will be able to do it, or … *nope!* This has to come from you.

Dig deep. We are mining, here... for a **brilliant GEM!**

Conceptualize | Session #17
The game changer

Create your own brainstorming list now for your brilliant goal—one idea that outshines the rest for improving your personal and/or professional life. Remember to take into account actions that either incorporate your other goals or help you accomplish them at the same time. The catch is—you have to be able to do it in ninety days. Achieving this benchmark should scare you but not overwhelm you. If it overwhelms you, choose a new one. If it scares you or makes you feel a little nervous, you have found the right one!

What is your brilliant goal? Write it down. That act alone is an attempt to hold yourself accountable for getting it done. It makes you much more likely to follow through.

Next, let's get to the *how.* You are going to create a plan for the next ninety days. While you may have started with a dream, deciding you can do that thing within the short time window moves it closer to reality. How will you do it? I'll show you. We are going to *reverse engineer* it.

While going through this process, if you realize your brilliant goal is not achievable, or it's too easy, or it conflicts with other personal goals you may have, it's not the right goal. If it's going to take you away from your family for too long, or stick you to a desk instead of working out, or shortchange another goal, it's not the right goal. If you reach this realization, I am going to ask you to stop and look back at your brainstorming list. Will anything else on there make a better brilliant goal? If it's not worth it to you, go back and rework this exercise.

Once you're sure, write your brilliant goal with confidence.

You've just sealed a deal with yourself.

Conceptualize | Session #18
the details

Brainstorm all of the things you "can do and/or need to do" to reach this brilliant end goal. Write them all down to every nitty-gritty detail.

Then with each of the things you wrote down, break those down into steps, if needed. Each step should take you twenty minutes or less. If a step will take longer, break it down into smaller steps. This is how you stick with a goal—by succeeding in small wins on the way toward winning the larger end game.

List every single thing. You are going to complete two of these small tasks per day, five days a week. That's just forty minutes or less daily, making progress toward your brilliant goal. Don't worry, we've already thought of ways to free up some extra time!

You have a full list to make progress. That way you won't have to think about *what* to do, only *when* to do it. Now, organize that list. Rewrite it before you go to bed tonight, in order. Then you won't have to worry about what and when—just doing what you've set forth.

> This list is your pattern for the next ninety days. You have just designed your life! Celebrate that, all by itself.

Now, you have one brilliant goal and nine other GEM goals. You have taken those gems and broken them down into actionable steps you estimate can be done in about twenty minutes.

But let's put all of those little moves into perspective. How do they, and your larger goal, fit into your future?

Remember Jack Johnson's song and **don't waste time on what won't move you forward.**

> For every decision you make from here on out, consider how it will play into where you want to be in five years.

Conceptualize | Session #19
rewards

You have to give each of your goals a due date. Then, plan how you will celebrate when you accomplish them. That's some powerful motivation. It can be something as simple as indulging in a bubble bath or making a date with a busy friend. When you make your schedule, be sure to set aside time for appreciating your own hard work.

Start writing down deadlines for each micro task, and for the completion of your larger GEM goals. These will be within ninety days, but you'll be able to finish many of them sooner. This means you're going to have some serious celebration time in the next three months! How will you fill it? Go ahead and write down your ideas.

Now that you're fired up, renew your commitment to work on these things. Only you can care enough to make yourself do the work. I once went to a conference and attended a talk by motivational speaker Simon Bailey. He told everyone in the room to raise their right hand and say, "The only hand that will ever feed me *is this one!*" His point? You have to decide to be self-reliant.

And you will! You've created your killer five-year plan. You've created your brilliant goal and nine other GEM goals. Now, *you do you.*

Get cracking!

Five

THE FINE ART OF SCHEDULING

THE FINE ART
OF SCHEDULING

"I don't want to get to the end of my life and find that I just lived the length of it. I want to have lived the width of it as well."
—Diane Ackerman

Time is our most valuable asset, yet it's the one we squander the most. This is because we haven't scheduled out our lives in larger blocks. We wait to react to what's going on around us instead of creating a schedule for our time and being both strict and flexible with it, as events warrant.

We also have different stages in life when this fluctuates. In high school, my life was so scheduled that when I got to college, the last thing I wanted was a timetable. I wanted to be wild and free. Then, after graduating, I realized I needed a schedule or I'd never get anything done. Now, as an entrepreneur, I understand the need for a formal agenda more than ever. I must time block, or I will spend the entire day working on what's in front of me or replying to emails. I'll feel so unproductive at the end of the day because **I spent those hours reacting, instead of being proactive.**

Creating a plan requires a schedule. Some of us overschedule. That's okay. It's called being ambitious. Others find a schedule daunting, but I'm here to tell you it doesn't have to be difficult to fall into the habit of checking things off your to-do list. In fact: it feels great.

Let's start with your ideal schedule. If everything was perfect and you were doing exactly what you wanted to do, what would it look like? Now, lower your expectations to what you *can* reasonably do. You can accomplish a lot in twenty-four hours. People do it all the time!

> "Don't say you don't have enough time. You have exactly the same number of hours per day that were given to Helen Keller, Pasteur, Michelangelo, Mother Teresa, Leonardo da Vinci, Thomas Jefferson, and Albert Einstein."
> – H. Jackson Brown, Jr.

Conceptualize | Session #20
ideal schedule

Don't chase someone else's idea of a dream schedule. Dig deep and figure out what you would want. I absolutely love working, so I would want to spend a good chunk of hours taking care of business every day. On the other hand, one of my dear friends hates showing up for a job day in and day out, so if she got to decide, she would be a stay-at-home mom most of the time. What's your preference? If you're running a business, we already have an idea of what it is.

Did you know we each have a most productive time of day? This is why we don't jump out of bed and vacuum or start a big research project at dinnertime. Besides just being practical, **there are secrets to perfect timing.**

According to Daniel H. Pink in his book *When*, one in every four people has a differing chronotype—the fancy word for your internal clock. Those with a standard chronotype experience the morning peak, afternoon trough and evening rebound; however, there are two others: the *night owl* and the early-rising *lark*. He goes on to describe three types of people by chronotype.

In Pink's reckoning, about one in five people are Larks—those who get to bed early and get up early. Their whole cycle through the day's energy peak, afternoon trough or low, and rebound happens a few hours earlier than average. These folks are more likely to be introverts. They also are seen as stable, happy, agreeable types.

A similar percentage of people are Owls, among whom are productive souls like inventor Thomas Edison and novelist Gustave Flaubert. Their body clocks run later than average, peaking at about 9 P.M. They work late into the night, trail off, and enjoy their rebound—conveniently—in the morning. Studies group Owls as creative thinkers and impulsive actors, who are less positive and consistent than their Lark counterparts.

Pink calls the rest of us *Third Birds*. A typical American workday revolves around the average productive time of Third Birds—about three of every five people—between 8 A.M. and 5 P.M. The rise and fall of their energy levels literally dictate the work schedules of most Americans in traditional jobs.

But you may have a choice. If you run your own business or choose a job outside the usual office timetable, you can take advantage of your own peak work time.

Conceptualize | Session #21

morning lark. night owl. third bird

To make the most out of your day, identify your chronotype. This will help you schedule your tasks as efficiently as possible.

I am an Owl, personally, so my greatest mental and physical energy occurs at night. Most of this book was written between the hours of 8 P.M. and 2 A.M. I have always experienced my most creative moments late at night or when I'm in the shower. I find this is my best place to think without distraction, and the time spent without my face in front of a computer screen or in meetings is definitely what's needed to get the creative juices flowing.

Pink emphasizes in his book no matter who you are, you need to try to schedule the mindless, busy-work tasks during the troughs—those times when high energy is waning and not yet rebuilding. If you're trying to get a favorable decision from someone, always try to book a morning appointment, then work off of your own "bird" type to schedule the rest of your day.

There is so much to discover about ourselves, isn't there? But once you understand yourself better and can plan around your ideal productivity time, you'll be better able to tackle life. Successful scheduling means you take out other distractions during each time block. You remove the distractions that come with doing "all of the things, all the time."

Conceptualize | Session #22
prioritizing

Let's return to what our ideal schedule looks like. Instead of gauging *what* you'd like to do, this time, you'll be focusing on schedule and timing. You only have so many hours in a day, so you must prioritize what is most important to you. Then, you have to figure out the best place to spend your time.

Prioritizing is all about cutting your losses and capitalizing on your strengths. Maybe you can cut something out of your life that has been taking up too much time and energy. Maybe you need to add something to your schedule you hadn't realized you wanted before.

You can't just make a few minor adjustments and get there. Things will not change if you do it that way. You have to step back and reconstruct your life. Then, stick to the new schedule for at least four weeks before you can evaluate how well it's working. You might need to move things around to better serve yourself.

To get started, say,

> "Today I am going to reevaluate my life. I am going to do this differently. I am going to make a plan that works best for me."

Wouldn't it be crazy if you got to do all of the things you wanted to do... and you *didn't* have to do the things you hate doing? Or no longer want to do? What would that even look like?

We rely on habits to save time. But needs and priorities change, so we must question whether old habits are still viable. Consider what you want to be doing five years from now. What do you want your life to look like? What changes do you need to make in order to get there?

Write it all down. If you have the *OWN IT* workbook, you'll find a lot of questions to help you discover your ideal schedule. If you don't, grab a notebook and write down what your ideal day looks like—during the week and on the weekend. Does your to-do list vary day-to-day? What time do you wake up, what time do you go to bed, and what happens in between?

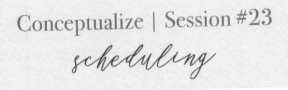

Conceptualize | Session #23

scheduling

Get out your calendar. If you have a physical planner or calendar, put pen to paper. If you prefer to go paperless, use your computer, phone app, or an online calendar and start to schedule things out. Begin with your essentials, then build out blocks of time (for work, leisure, family, etc.). Then narrow it down more. Keep in mind your chronotype!

Each day, I try to carve out a little bit of time for each of these: work, leisure, and family. Then, I label each of those slots with what I should be doing during those periods. This way I only have to focus on one thing during that time, instead of "all of the things," (which never works).

For example, on Mondays, during work time in the morning (my personal rebound period), I schedule out the rest of the week, plan for any meetings I have, and get ready for what is to come. I try to schedule all my meetings for Tuesdays. I know on any given Tuesday I will have a line-up of meetings to attend, and I will have to work backwards to prepare for them. Wednesday's work focus is social media planning for the week (Instagram, podcast, blog, etc.). Wednesday's top priority, though, is family "walk and explore" time. We usually take a long walk, go to the beach, or wander around a new place. Thursdays I focus on finalizing things for the week—any task that needs to get done. It is go time! I am ready to get answers, take action, and make magic happen. We are so close to the end of the week, I make sure to get as much done as possible. On Friday, the portion of the day that is family time is spent cleaning or organizing, so we can enjoy the rest of the weekend together without chores to do. On the weekends we have our leisure time and schedule time for coffee, dinner dates, and play dates with friends and family.

Time blocking

I have included a sample week in the *OWN IT* workbook to help you design what you want your weekly schedule to look like. If you are creative, like me, you will probably want to write it out and make it pretty. Have fun! Get out your paints, markers, colored pencils, and get to work. It's your life. Turn it into art. Making a schedule doesn't have to be daunting or put unreasonable demands on our time. Ultimately, by doing this, we are freeing ourselves to create more—to create beautiful moments, golden opportunities, efficiency, experiences, and memories. There is so much you can do when you make scheduling an art.

I'm not saying you need to literally take up painting or sculpting, but you do need to be the artist of your own life. You get to design it. Every moment of every day is ultimately up to you.

What will you do with it?

Conceptualize | Session #25
big picture

Now, back to the bigger picture:

- What do you think you'll want five years down the road?

- What are you going to focus on for the next five years to help you achieve or acquire it?

- Create one major focus for each year, to get you where you want to go.

This may feel like you are jumping the gun, but it's just a direction to start. We are not going to plan out all five years. However, the initial work will give you direction for the next five to come.

> You have to gaze toward the horizon to see the rainbows!

Next, you are going to map out the following year. Don't worry: there is also an art to this. Break down the year into three-month increments. (It's no accident that this fits well with your ninety-day goals.)

What will you focus on? Knowing your GEM goals, decide what project you will create and complete in those three months. Pair each goal you have with complementary projects meant to help you reach the ultimate brilliant goal.

Next you'll have to break down those projects into steps and what you will focus on each week. We practiced this in Chapter Four, so you're ready to apply what you've learned. Write these down. You will have four big projects this year to help you accomplish your goals. What will they be?

Finally, decide what you will do during each time of the year, and remember: timing matters. You will most likely want to put your biggest project at the beginning of the year, as this is usually when you will be most motivated. At the end of the year, you might get caught up in the holidays, so you could reserve that time for smaller projects. It all depends on what kind of lifestyle and business you have. You do you!

> "What you do today is important because you are exchanging a day of your life for it."
> —Elizabeth George

CHAPTER 6

find your focus.

FIND YOUR FOCUS

To create something exceptional, your mindset must be relentlessly focused on the smallest detail.
—Giorgio Armani

You now have defined success, decided on your purpose, written out your goals, and scheduled your days. All of this is absolutely incredible and a huge accomplishment. You are halfway through this book, and your life has been transformed. Before continuing onto this next chapter, it's time to celebrate with family and friends. Sometimes, it's great to celebrate by yourself with a glass of wine or a latte, a long bath, and some macarons—but not this time. Now that you have done the necessary solitary work, you can indulge in the support of your circle of friends and loved ones.

It's time to bring them into your endeavor: they are the ones you will ask to hold you accountable to living out this newly designed dream life. While you don't need their approval, you do need their observance. If they've got your back, you'll get where you want to go.

Why turn the important job of accountability over to others? Because life happens! There are going to be distractions, and you need to make sure to keep your focus.

Did you know that Coco Chanel, after much success in the fashion and perfume industries, shut down her business in 1939? There is a lot of controversy as to why, but ultimately, she closed down her couture house and didn't reappear in the fashion world until 1954 at the age of seventy-one. She made a major comeback and created the iconic Chanel suit that still lives on today.

She came back and *focused* on what she needed to do to make her comeback.

> No matter your age or experience, focus is key. No matter what you have been through or where you are going, if you concentrate on what you want—armed with specific goals and a great plan—you can achieve it.

Like Coco Chanel, you're on your way! You have created a pattern, or map, of what you want your gorgeous life to look like and where you want to go. You have narrowed down your key priority, and now is the time to focus.

Of course, you have to leave time to react to things that happen during the "whirlwind," but you also have to start setting aside time for these dreams you've made. You'll want to live and work less in the present whirlwind, and more in the realm of your future dreams.

I admit, focus does not come easy for me. When I close my eyes at night, to-do lists, new ideas, and shiny dreams fill my head. I rarely sleep more than six hours. I have a million things I want to do and tons of ideas about how I can get there. So my problem, as you can see, is focusing on one thing at a time. More often than not, when I'm awake, I am tempted to get caught up in the daily storm, where distractions are abundant. I also know I am the one who *creates* those blustery weather conditions.

The question becomes: how do I make it stop? How do I create order and engage in organization? With the details handled, I'll ultimately be able to focus on my priorities. In this chapter, we are going to discuss the ways in which you can get down to business to create less chaos and more *focus*. Stick with me. There are sunny skies ahead.

Where to begin?

Start by writing out the thoughts you currently have or have had in the past about setting or reaching goals. By doing this, you create organization in your mind and in the world around you. Separate what you have already considered and what needs to get done. This might take a while depending on whether you have taken notes on your ideas, but I promise, it will pay off in the end.

f. o. c. u. s.

Here is an acronym to help you *focus*.

F | Find time each day to work on your goals.
To do this, set aside time devoted solely to working toward your goals.

O | Old ways won't open new doors.
You will need to be creative in how you do things now. Don't just go through the same doors you have in the past.

C | Create new habits.
Make reminders and motivation easy and automatic. Set your phone alarm to tell you when to move on to the next task. Post your aspirations where you can see them every day.

U | Utilize your resources.
I'm sure you have resources at your fingertips you aren't using yet. It's time to take inventory of those, so you can reach for them when you need them.

S | Set yourself up for success.
Take away your distractions. Devise systems to avoid getting caught up in competing concerns. Set yourself up for success, stay organized, and focus on your key priority and the goals you have set for yourself.

The trickiest part about focusing? No one else can do it for you. Think of it as the space needed to do homework back in school. While you could ask for help, in the end, you had to do the reading, thinking, and problem solving needed to get that A. This is also true about life, no matter what industry or job you are in. Sure, there will be hard moments and decisions needing to be made, but ultimately you are the only one who can handle what is required.

Let me share a story with you on what focus can look like.

> "I'm driving toward the gunshots,
> I just wanted you to know I love you!"
>
> "No—don't go. Call somebody else!"
>
> "There is no one else. I'm it."

No, this dialogue is not from the latest Spielberg. It's actually a conversation I had with my husband. You see, it's his job to drive toward danger. In very dark contrast to my profession of event planning, my husband is a police officer. At that moment, gang members were shooting at his car. All I wanted was for him to turn around and drive away from danger, but he focused—he stayed. He did his job. And yes, thankfully and by the grace of God, he made it back home safely.

My husband and I balance each other out. I show him there is light and love in the world. He keeps me aware and alive. He loves rules. I push the rules to see if we can just go one step further (usually toward making things better—well, at least in my opinion). One thing our jobs do have in common is we have to face the hard stuff, head on. We have to commit. We have to focus.

As an entrepreneur, this was a tough lesson for me to learn. I was waiting for a business coach to tell me how to do it, or a friend or partner to say, "Well, if you did this or that, it would make a difference." I wanted someone else to tell me how to make my business better, to improve my workflow, or to find me the one client that would make business boom. The truth is, no one will. In a competitive marketplace, you—the business owner, the designer of your couture life—are the one and only person who will care the most.

You have to F.O.C.U.S. and do the hard stuff. Maybe you will secure the one client who will make all the difference, or a game-changing moment of luck will skyrocket your goals, but you can't count on that. You have to count on yourself (and the grace of God).

So let's face it, head on: today, I challenge you to tackle the task you have been avoiding, the job you have been procrastinating —perhaps from fear of starting.

Now is the time!

Conceptualize | Session #27
compile your notes

How do we organize our thoughts without relying on stacks of sticky notes, journals, and phone notes? Is there even a better way?

The answer isn't black and white. There are a lot of different ways to stay on track—to focus. The key? Find one system that works for you and stick with it. Choose one, just one.

> Staying organized is paramount. Like the tailoring of a couture gown, it must be done bit by bit— in order. It's meticulous work, but if you're organized, it will pay off in unimaginable ways.

Consider your written notes as pieces of that gown. Do you have them spread out on the virtual work table in front of you? The problem isn't taking notes in different places; it's forgetting where you put them and then losing them altogether in the shuffle when you want to go back to them. It seems so simple, but this discipline is hard. You have to train yourself to do it. Start now. Don't wait until tomorrow. Trust me on this one.

Let's clean house. Take every note you have related to your new plan— from scraps of paper, your phone files, your journal—and put them in one place. You will probably notice you have a few duplicates, which is usually an indication something is important to you. Prioritize these notes. Highlight them or mark each with a star. You may want to mull over these ideas first. Now, do you have your full list in one place? Start to organize and prioritize how and what you want to tackle first.

So often, we wait for the "right time" to complete something, or we think we'll come back to it when we have a "free" moment. Are there items on your list you can complete immediately? Are you alive and breathing? Do them now. Why wait another second? Open yourself up to be able to move onto the other, bigger things.

FOCUS *on your goals*

What follows below are four steps that need to be done today. These starting points will change the way you do business, help you handle things directly, and F.O.C.U.S.

Tailor it down. You might not be able to do everything on your list today or this week, so you must decide what will make the biggest difference in meeting your goals right now. Next, make a list for this month, then for this year. Then list out the things you might want to think about next year, or in the next five years, on a different list. Keep a master file.

Tailoring down all of your ideas and to-do's so you have a concise *must-do* list for today, this week, and this month will make a huge difference in your daily focus.

VISIONARY PLANNING

1. Set your monthly goals:
   - Take your ninety-day goals from Chapter 4.
   - Take your compiled notes from Brainstorm Session #2, above.
   - Now break your goals down by month.
2. Set your daily goals:
   - At the beginning of each week, create a daily goal list. I

like to do this on Sundays or Mondays. I set aside time to make goals for each day of the upcoming week. Make your daily goal list first thing in the morning, when you wake up—before you check your email or answer a phone call. Writing them down first sets them in stone. It prevents you from forgetting or avoiding them. It holds you accountable.

3. Create a to-do list:

- Look at your set-in-stone daily goals, and create a to-do list. Do it in an environment that is calming and safe for you. This means if you have children, you can't be making your to-do list while trying to get them ready for school. You'll need to wake up before them, get your coffee, and make your list. As much as we may hate structure, we need it. Structure builds systems and processes that help us get where we want to go. And boy, do we love that!

4. Prioritize:

- Now that you have your full to-do list, prioritize your tasks by writing numbers next to them. Start with the items that may take you the longest to start, or are the hardest, and do the easy tasks last. Why? If you aren't able to complete something today, you have only easy things to add to your list for tomorrow.

So many times, when entrepreneurs get to this point we feel overwhelmed: we now have goals and a huge to-do list, but we don't really know where to start or what will be most important. The question then becomes: where do we focus our time, energy, and money when they are all limited resources?

Let's consider for a moment what it is that makes *you* valuable.

Entrepreneurs tend to believe because we own the business, we have to do it all. While I do believe you have to take ownership over every aspect, you can't possibly *do* it all by yourself. And you certainly cannot do it all by yourself, *all at once.* So what needs your personal attention?

There is something unique about you that makes you who you are. You have brought this into your business, and it's why your business is successful. If your business is not successful yet, it's time to ask yourself, what part of your business is *you?*

There are so many areas of your business on which you can spend your time. You need to narrow it down and focus on the things that *only you* can do. This includes the areas that bring you joy.

The only thing someone else cannot do in your business for you is *be you.* You have to put yourself into your brand in order to make it successful. The separation of personal life and business is important, but in order to grow, to do what you do best, your business has to be infused with your personality and perspective—it's what makes you who you are.

The more you own your niche—the way you show what is truly, genuinely, authentically *you* through what you do—the more you will attract the exact clients you want. That's how you'll grow the business and become who you want to become: the person that "seven-year-old you" always wanted to be.

Like all lessons, I learned this the hard way.

Why does it seem like all of our most vulnerable moments happen in the bathroom, of all places? This story very literally took place in the restroom, a super fancy restroom, but a restroom nonetheless. Specifically, in *the stall* of the fancy restroom.

Here we are, setting up for a client's dream day, and I am taking a break for just a moment. I run to the restroom. I'm in the stall, I've locked the door, and before my pants hit the floor, the florist walks in with one of her assistants. I recognize her voice. Mind you, this is a florist I have admired since I started planning weddings and a client hired her. I am over the moon we are finally working on a project together.

As they walk into the restroom her assistant remarks, "This coordination team is really sweet." I smile to myself in delight. *They like us, too!* Soon after, to my utter devastation, the florist replies, "Yeah, but a little too sweet... this girl is too young and has no idea what she is doing. She is all glitter and pink tulle." My heart sank.

I had two options. I could walk out of the stall, say hello, and then take whatever came next. Or I could sit down on the toilet as quietly as possible, pull up my feet in silence, and hide.

I did the latter... I sat there, on the toilet, and listened as they bashed our company, my dignity, and my feelings. I was crushed. Sure, I *was* young. And yes, I *did* love pink and glitter, but there was no pink tulle at *this* wedding. I could do any type of wedding! She'd put me in a box: a pink box wrapped up with a gold, glittery bow.

Before I realized what a beautiful gift this was, I set out to prove her wrong and show the world I could do any kind of wedding. I took every kind of wedding job I could find. I even took a steampunk wedding. I had to Google "steampunk" while I sat in the initial meeting, but then said... *yes, of course!*

I was just starting out in that first year, and I ended up with only four weddings. I discounted, sold myself short, and begged for couples to like me. I tried to hang out with the "cool vendors," hoping someone would refer me. I worked hard at making our website diverse by showing all of the different styles of weddings and events we could do.

Remember back in junior high? Our greatest fear was not fitting in! But then, who are the cool kids? Those who *stand out.*

> What if we have to make ourselves vulnerable
> to stand out and be accepted?

Yes, we are going to have humiliating bathroom moments. Yes, we are going to have people who don't choose us because we don't create weddings or events that are their style. But you have to come to a point where, when you lose a client or a job because it's not your style, you say, "Great," and move on. We don't *want* to do every wedding! We want clients that love us because our style matches theirs—we have similar values and like-minded aesthetics, and they trust us because of it.

To get anywhere in this business, we have to stand out. We have to be "different" and offer something unique from our competition. If we don't, we will just fit in and fade into the scenery.

So, now, this comes down to *you.* In my business, I tried so hard to be who "they" wanted us to be. But if you put *you* back into your brand, you will go so much further. Remember, "You do you."

Think back to when you were eleven years old, before the bullies of junior high told you different was wrong, when you were your most creative, true self. You were most likely truly and authentically yourself because you didn't worry about being different. No one had broken you down yet, no one had told you that you couldn't do things that way, or that you were weird.

Focus on that girl—seven-year-old you. Who is she? She is still inside you. While she is older and more refined now, sometimes we need to bring out that seven-year-old. She was real, authentic, alive, and oh, so beautiful. She had big dreams, she was creative, and she was doing things "her way." It's astonishing to me how many times we push away that girl because, now, people have told us we should do things differently or because we see others doing them differently. I want you to take a moment and go back to that young self. Focus on what seven-year-old you would want, what she has to offer your business, what awesomeness she could bring to the table. Then, let her do just that!

Finding yourself will also help you create a more authentic and real brand. And even though your brand may not represent you exactly, or maybe you are trying to reach a different market, you still need to insert yourself into your business.

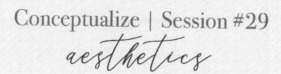

Conceptualize | Session #29
aesthetics

Now take out a pen and paper, and write down these two things:

1. Personal aesthetic
2. Brand values and aesthetics

What is your personal aesthetic? This is your taste, style, look, and feel. It underlies and guides your work, your business, and your life.

You may already know what yours is. If not, ask friends. Ask someone who will tell you the truth. They should know what they think of when they attempt to describe you.

I didn't want to be pink and fluffy—I felt like pink and fluffy was broken, wrong, or bad because that's what the world had told me when I started to grow up. When I asked others, they told me I was light, bright, cotton candy. I had to honor that side of myself and realize that while I may have *tried* to stifle that girl in me for a little while, "seven-year-old me" was still going to be there.

How do you figure out your personal aesthetic? Think about where you like to shop. Are you preppy J.Crew? Quirky, unique Anthropologie? Hip Urban Outfitters? Or, what character are you in a classic movie? Whose style do you most closely align with?

Aesthetics are great—they all work—you just have to pick one theme! When we try to be too many things to too many people, we lose our style. We have to really dig into the nitty gritty and focus on what we want our brand to look like moving forward. When you try too hard to have multiple aesthetics, saying by default that you're "eclectic," that's when things get uncoordinated and just don't work.

Now, focus on your brand's values and aesthetic. Is there anything different from you for your brand? What does your brand value? What is your brand's style?

Write this all out, as fast as you can: don't overthink it.

Usually, your personal aesthetic and your brand aesthetic are going to be similar. Or at the very least they should be somewhat related, since that is who you are and who you can best be as a brand.

I have met a few incredible business owners whose brand values and aesthetics were different from their personal ones, and that is okay. Make sure, if this is the case, you have made a clear distinction. You may have some crossover, but you need to decide and be crystal clear about what each looks like.

Why? What you put out into the world is what you are going to get back.

For me, once I embraced my cotton candy aesthetic, everything changed! I found "my people, my tribe, and my brides." I attracted the soft, romantic, "pretty" weddings full of pinks, blushes, and golds. I felt the most alive and creative when working with these clients. They were sweet and oh so kind. They understood my aesthetic and my style and loved them. Seriously, it was a match made in heaven.

When I owned it, I went from doing four weddings in the first year (when I was trying to please everyone and throw steampunk weddings) to forty weddings my second year! We have expanded and have coordinators working up the coast of California, from San Diego to San Francisco and we are now branching into international events.

What I didn't understand at first was if I was real, authentic, and completely myself, these brides, other vendors, and clients I was trying to impress would actually like me *more*. People sense when you are just telling them what they want to hear. When it comes from inside you, all questions of your sincerity fade away.

What about you? What do you love? Have you been holding back because you are afraid someone might not like what you love? Instead, concentrate on all of those who *will* love it!

Suppose we didn't copy what the other "big players" in our industry were doing. What if we only showed what we loved and what we found to be the prettiest, and waited to see what happened?

Look back again at your younger selves. Look at you when you were eight, twelve, or sixteen, and compare them to *this* you. **Have you dulled yourself a bit?** Maybe, occasionally, that could be a good thing. But I would say, for the most part, you have done yourself a disservice by restricting yourself to only what others want you to do. You can do incredible things at any age, but only when you have the courage to be who you are—to not only fit in, but to create something that is uniquely yours.

I often feel I can be my most authentic self with my longtime best friend, Nicole. You know, that friend you have known since grade school. She's the one who knows the silly, wacky, quirky sides of me fewer people got to know after I entered the intimidating locker room of middle school.

Nicole and I have walked the mall halls with Spice Girl hairstyles, adorning butterfly clips, glitter eyes, and cat ears. With her I just feel free to 'be'... to laugh, to cry, to tell her the truth about how I am feeling because I know she knows my heart completely and fully. There is no judgment but she will tell me straight up when I am being crazy or if I am wrong, yet she still has my back. What if we all lived this way as adults and we could be our most true, authentic selves without fear of judgment? What would you be doing differently? Why not take the leap and try it! Be fearless.

To find what makes your brand unique, go back and put *you* back into your business. It may seem silly and elementary, but that unvarnished element of personality is going to be the thing that makes the biggest difference.

People can smell real, and they can also sniff out a façade, real fast.

So just show and own who you really are. In my office, you can usually find glitter or confetti on the floor. People point out I have it stuck to my face or my clothes, too. Before I embraced my true self, I would have tried to brush it off, or sweep it under the rug. But not anymore!

Take pride in your work. Do it with the style you love. Care about the little things, do them the way they should be done, with integrity... and get ready to be surprised. Trust me, there is someone out there who wants what only you can create. When you are *most* yourself is when you and your brand will thrive!

So to wrap up this chapter, in a pink, pretty bow—beauty comes from the inside out. That's also true of your brand.

CHAPTER
seven

BUILDING YOUR TRIBE.

BUILD YOUR TRIBE

Your tribe is the most important part of your business. This includes the people who root for you, the people who work for you, and the people you work for—your clients. You've already begun the process of attracting the people who root for you, so let's dive into the other two.

When I was in college, I had the opportunity to intern at *San Diego Magazine*, where I did exactly as they told me: I entered the data they gave me, and got coffee when they asked. Little did I know the young woman next to me, also an intern, was writing articles for the magazine. No one asked her to, but this was something she really wanted to do, so she just did it. She went above and beyond. She did *more* than what was asked of her, and then she submitted her writing. I didn't know this until after our internship ended and I saw an article she had written published in the magazine. I found out she had been offered a job at the magazine after our internship ended *because she went the extra mile.* I now tell this story to each of our interns when they first start, to let them know I will take notice and they can make themselves stand out by seeing what's needed and *doing it.* It's really that simple.

To prove this point, our former intern at my event planning company, Karina, is now a profit-share partner. She worked her way up in the business. She started as an intern and she made herself indispensable! She would see things that needed to be done and do them before she was asked or told. She was a catch-all worker who never hesitated to get the job done. When I would say, "Okay, next we have to…" she would reply, "Saw it on the list and did it." Do you know how valuable that is to a business leader?

As her internship came to a close I realized I didn't want to work without her. She volunteered to do another semester of the internship to gain more experience while she finished school (once again going above and beyond). Nearing the end of her senior year, as she started to apply for jobs, I knew I needed her on our team. I asked if she would be interested in working for Couture Events full time. I said she could start as my assistant but over time create her own position and grow with the company. She said, "Yes."

Karina assisted me and "saved" me so many times. She kept me organized and on top of things and was transparent with me, letting me know when she was ready to move up. Karina soon became a coordinator, and then lead coordinator over our team as it began to grow. She supported me in countless ways, and when the business grew, I wanted to offer her something more, which is where profit-sharing came in. Instead of giving up equity in my company, I offered her a portion of the profits for as long as she is with us. We both won. I granted her the ability to invest even more energy in the business and to see a greater return that would benefit both her and the company. She now handles finances, timelines, budgets, vendor communications, etc.—things that at one point I wanted to do by myself. Was that the most wise use of my time and energy? Not really. Giving someone else the opportunity to create a role for themselves and grow with the company was one of the most valuable things I could have done in the delegation department.

While I do want you to own every aspect of your business, I know it's impossible to *do* every aspect of your business. **Newsflash: *you must delegate.***

But what do you delegate? How much do you give away? To whom do you delegate, and how do you know you can trust them? How do you know when you can afford to do this? The truth is, you can't afford *not* to.

I have seen so many business owners wear all of the hats. While this will work for a certain amount of time, as your business expands, you will not be able to meet your growing workload and demands. To even try to handle it all alone puts you at serious risk of dropping the ball, or worse, burning yourself out.

So, why not set yourself up for success now? We'll start, as we have in each chapter thus far, by digging a bit deeper.

building your tribe
(and delegating to them)

It's time to ask yourself: what do you *want* to do?

Which aspects of your business and your day-to-day do you love doing? Write them down, and then add the tasks you dread doing.

Now, think about the things that *only you* can do when it comes to your company. What sets your business apart? Those qualities are probably related to your individual voice and abilities. Write down the things only you can do and the reasons why.

Next, take a moment and look back through your list. What could you potentially let go of, but still oversee?

Last, but not least, let's evaluate your strengths and weaknesses. Are you really good at some of the things you like to do? Is there someone who could do them better? Be honest about your assets and liabilities. Consider asking the opinion of those who know you best. DO NOT let your weaknesses get to you... everyone has them, even Superman. Just start by writing them all down.

After making your two lists, go through and mark the tasks and aspects of your business a new hire could take care of for you. Think about it this way: if you had the money to hire one more person, who would you hire? What use of human resources would make the biggest difference for your business? Better yet, is there anything that would remove a huge weight from your shoulders?

Just one person can make all the difference in your workflow. This will instantly improve your ability to focus on your top business priorities.

When looking through all aspects of my business years ago, I realized I needed help with finances. I knew nothing about accounting or bookkeeping. That was the main pain point in my enterprise; all of my frustrations came back to the money. So, I did it. I took the leap and hired a bookkeeper. This worked for a while, but eventually I started facing problems again. My business wasn't turning a profit, and I didn't understand why.

When I delegated responsibility to my new bookkeeper, I went full hands-off. I wanted her to just take care of it. I didn't want to learn the money side of the business—knowing why or what my new hire was doing was uninteresting. And frankly, that's why I hired her, right? Not so.

After several months, I was talking with a friend, and she shared her horrific story about getting audited. What's more: *her bookkeeper was my bookkeeper!*

That moment drove home an important point. Even when delegating to others, it was crucial *I* still learned, understood, and monitored what they were doing and how they were doing it. That was my obligation as a business owner.

As much as I wanted to be blissfully ignorant in this area of my organization, it was not benefiting me. I still needed to own it. I could and should let someone else take care of my finances, but I needed to oversee them. I needed to be shown monthly profit and loss statements. Ultimately, I am always accountable for my finances being handled correctly. The United States Treasury and Internal Revenue Service would agree.

Maintaining ownership while delegating specific tasks to others is a useful skill. Once you establish a solid level of trust with your new hire (base this on proven quality of his/her work), a great way to keep ownership is to have your team put together daily or weekly reports on their deliverables, accomplishments, opportunities, and upcoming work. Keep an open conversation, and schedule regular check-ins to keep everyone on track and in the loop.

Now you've identified what you like and dislike, what you can delegate and what you need to keep. Now look back at your lists. What is one thing you need to do yourself? What is one thing you could ask someone to do? Could you hire an assistant and have them take on multiple tasks?

For me, after onboarding an accountant, hiring an assistant was next on my list.

Pro tip: Consider personal assistance a top-notch option when you're just starting out on your own. You can delegate combined personal and business tasks like picking up dry cleaning and going grocery shopping, as well as helping with the company's admin work, sorting emails, mailing packages, etc. Hire for what you need most.

To find a personal assistant, I headed back to my university alma mater. I was looking for someone reliable, flexible, kind, and organized. Students need money and are often looking for part-time work—a great option for them and me. For people resources, think about communities you are or have been involved in. Use networks such as your church, university, online forum, summer camp—go ahead and stretch to find different pools of candidates. Put the word out you are looking for someone.

Before you begin interviewing, list the attributes of the perfect new hire. This will help you decide where to look and what to look for. Ultimately, it will help you weed out unfit candidates quickly.

If you are looking for someone to only help with one aspect of your business, narrow the candidate pool at universities by focusing on specific majors. Or, start asking people from other industries who don't mind sharing their knowledge and lessons learned with you. For example, if I needed help with graphic design, I could post on a university board and ask for only graphic design major students. I could ask other business owners to share the name of the person who created their fabulous logo for them.

There is also this wonderful thing called the World Wide Web. I have discovered some of my most talented contractors from around the world online. You'll find a roster of online resources in the back of this book.

One last thing: consider looking into a virtual assistant (VA) to help you with administrative tasks and emails. I personally like to know my assistant and meet face-to-face at least once a week, but lots of entrepreneurs have virtual assistance performed from around the world to take care of everyday tasks for them. The VAs are usually more affordable as well. Consider the tasks you want them to do, and then decide if you need someone who is with you in person or if a VA could work for you.

While you are probably very excited about the potential of passing off some things in your business, you still have a lot of work to do in order to get the business organized and to a place where you can hire help. If you just turn work over to someone, I promise, you will be firing them or redoing their work within the next month... probably because "they aren't doing it right." The truth is, if that happens, it is likely your fault. Before you can start to delegate, you must create action steps or standard operating procedures (SOPs) from which others will work. These procedures provide the boundaries that are needed as businesses grow. Bringing in outside help provides a lot of potential, but also a myriad of ways to interpret your orders or requests. Your SOPs give your people a working roadmap.

Want things done your way? Prefer that employees design their own work plans? Whichever you choose, you must give them a manual, or a way you want things done. List every step. This is how to ensure work is completed consistently and accurately. If you are turning over some of your computer or online tasks, you can take screen captures or make video recordings to show them, step-by-step, how you do things. As an entrepreneur you don't want to be told what to do but "worker bees" are happiest when they are told exactly how to do it. They want guidance and are looking to you to give it to them. You need to change your mindset and put yourself in their shoes. They don't want to "figure it out," they need step-by-step direction.

In my own business, I even created templated emails that can be filled in and customized as needed. The templates provide direction and a place to start the response. I know this may seem daunting, but in the long run, it will save you so much time. Apart from your tribe, time is arguably your most valuable asset.

In addition to preparing instructions, it's time to organize the "tools" your new hire will need. For instance, which files, products, and information will help them do their job? Set them up for success and reduce everyone's frustration by centralizing the things they need to fulfill their duties. When I hired my first assistant, I was flustered she didn't know which weddings we had already featured on our blog and social media and which ones we hadn't. I asked her to look through all of our posts to find out.

Now, looking back, I realize my request was a bit... well... ridiculous. I had asked her to do the organizing *and* to get everything in the right file for each of our clients. "Just ask me if you need direction," I told her. Well, that was a guaranteed way to waste time.

The end result? It took us longer to get organized than it would have if I had prepared in advance. Ultimately, I lost time and resources. I ended up letting her go and doing it all myself again. I felt like no one else could do it right. Had it gone on much longer, she would probably have left on her own, thinking I could never be satisfied.

You must think about the things only you know right now, and start to get them organized so this information is easily communicated or found when needed. Here's an example of how I made this work after learning the lesson the hard way. Before I hired my next assistant, I created a file-sharing system in Dropbox for our business, with a file for each client, categorized by labels: current, needs to be featured, and already featured. I separated out our editorial shoots, real weddings, and events. I did the pre-work so she could jump right in with the real work we needed to get done.

> Systems and processes are key to building a team.
> You must get organized before you grow.

I had the opportunity to plan the wedding of Leigh Keith, co-founder (with her brother, Bill Keith) of Perfect Bar, a whole-foods nutrition snack company. The siblings' story is incredible: their father, Bud, came up with the original recipe and sold the nutrition bars to sport teams to support their family of fifteen. When Bud became ill with skin cancer and passed away, the oldest siblings knew they had to figure out a way to provide for their family. They turned their dad's recipe into a business. In just twelve years, they took the traveling business from their family van (their headquarters while growing up) to over twelve thousand stores nationwide... and still growing. They have crushed the competition and overcome what seemed to be unfortunate circumstances. Talk about inspiring!

After getting to know Leigh and spending time with her and her sister Charisse, I asked if they would speak at our Confetti Conference—the gathering for creative women entrepreneurs (www.confettiinc. com/confetti-conference). At this conference, we bring in the best of the best from different industries to join together and learn from one other. These like-minded women generate immense power in this intimate setting, encouraging attendees to accomplish brilliant goals, take their businesses to the next level, and transform their daily grind and hustle into a productive and clear vision. The Keiths were a perfect fit as speakers to this audience. They said yes, along with business strategist Jasmine Star, profit coach Danielle Mulvey, and Ali Grant, founder of Be Social, as our key speakers.

During the conference, all of the speakers and panelists were sharp and relevant, but one piece of information Leigh and Charisse shared with us was invaluable. In particular, Charisse said something that will always stand out for me. As the company's Chief Operations Officer, she is responsible for getting their operations approved.

When the time came for an approval request, Charisse identified the many SOPs they had on file at Perfect Bar, and walked her inquisitors through the procedures they had put in place. And then... they asked for the SOP's SOPs. "What?" she exclaimed. Charisse had no idea that standard operating procedures needed *their own* SOPs. But, yes, that is how important they are. Looking back, Charisse understood exactly why they were needed: standardized operations and procedures are important requirements in the food industry—people's health and safety are at stake.

My pitch to you is this: SOPs should be equally important in every industry. Clearly defined standard operating procedures will help your company run like a well-oiled machine. The stronger your SOPs, the more hands-off you can be, the more safely you can delegate to others, and the less risk you assume.

Please give these your attention when beginning your business. If you don't, you will regret it, and you'll have to go back and do it later anyway. Thinking ahead and preparing will make a huge difference for you and your company. It may feel like a daunting task to get organized, but trust me, it will give you freedom.

Conceptualize | Session #31
leading your tribe

You've hired some new faces. You've empowered them with the right instructions for getting work done. But just telling people what to do isn't enough. Now, *how* will you lead?

Being a leader is difficult. In my years of doing business, I have found the best leaders lead by example. We dive in. When at an event, I am the one out at the venue doing the prep work, moving what needs to be moved, and making it all happen.

I am not just a pointer. I am a doer. I not only *tell* folks how to do things, but I also *show* them.

This is an essential element to success for us. My team sees I am willing to get my hands dirty at a wedding or event and—in the future—I hope they, too, will do what needs to be done to complete the job to perfection.

At one of our weddings in a gorgeous winery in Napa, California, the guys who laid the dance floor, over grass, were three feet off center. They were about three-quarters of the way done when I was able to take measurements. I asked them to move the dance floor to the right spot. They stared at me like I was crazy. The leader of the rental team said, "Ma'am, we can't move it." I looked at them, looked back at my team, and said, "Well, if they can't, I will." Both the vendor team and my own team watched in amazement as I started to move the dance floor piece by piece, deconstructing what they had just put together. I did it kindly and courteously, of course, but it had to be done. Soon, my team snapped out of it, realized I was serious, and started to help me. After moving ten pieces of dance floor, the rental lead said, "Okay, okay, I guess we can do it."

I have countless other examples of being proactive. I believe in doing the job right and making sure it's perfect, even if it means working longer and harder. Our clients expect the best, and that is what we are going to give them. My point is, leaders who aren't willing to do the nitty-gritty themselves can't expect their teams to do it. You must lead by example and show them how, not just tell them.

> Nothing is impossible. It might take extra time and effort, but our work must be done right, or why do it at all?

I instill this in my team and in our tribe.

Conceptualize | Session #32
ideal client—tribal fit

Now that you have worked on building and leading your tribe, let's work on building your following: your clients. This is the second aspect of your tribe. To begin building your client base, you must first pinpoint who you are looking to attract. You must define your ideal client.

It's time to sit down and write out exactly who your ideal client is, every detail you can possibly imagine about him/her/them. To reach your ideal client, you must relate to them, and to relate to them, you must know who they are.

Where do they live? How old are they? Where do they work (if they work)? Where do they spend their free time? What type of vehicle do they drive? What's their favorite color? And so on. You can explore this more in your *OWN IT* workbook, or by making a list in your journal.

Next, you need to start marketing *only* to this person. You may be thinking, "But I want to reach more people! I have multiple ideal clients." The truth is, if you market to everyone, you will reach no one. If you find a niche client you begin marketing toward, you will find your tribe, and they will respond to you.

Name your ideal client. For my event coordination business, Couture Events, our ideal client's name is "Elle." When Elle first came to life, my team and I started to ask ourselves, what does Elle want? If you can answer this single question, you can then start to solve her problem, which is how you satisfy clients.

Stop marketing in the same way your competition is marketing. To stand out, you have to do something different. You have to write your own story and mind your own business.

> Stop looking at everyone else's stories
> and begin selling your own.

Spend some more time thinking about how you will "marry" your ideal client with your unique product or service. This will give you a glimpse into an effective marketing direction.

CHAPTER

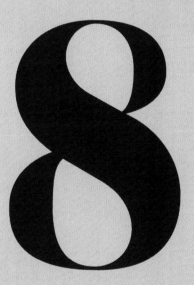

REVIEW, REFINE, EDIT, GET AFTER IT!

"Never give up on a dream just because of the time it will take to accomplish it. The time will pass anyway."
—Earl Nightingale

You have done a lot of hard work to get to this point. Now, here's the kicker: you need to analyze your progress every three months.

Conceptualize | Session #33

review

It's time to reevaluate! Look at where you've been, what you've done, what's working, and what's not working. Take everything into consideration when reviewing. Be ready to let go of what is no longer working or what no longer serves you, in order to figure out what is next to come. Earlier in my career I had a bridal gown retail shop for three years but after reviewing (and much help from my business coach), I realized I had to choose what I invested my time into and I had to look at it from a business perspective. He said to me, "Krystel, you can do anything you set your mind to but you can't do everything. What are you going to choose?" I really wanted to do it all but I needed to be wise with the time I had. This was a hard lesson to learn but sometimes you have to let things go that are no longer working or serving you. I was having a baby and while I wanted to do it all, I also needed to think about the time I was going to devote to my new priority.

Marcus Lemonis, host of the CNBC show *The Profit,* does this with each new company he attains. He instructs management to identify their least-sold products or services... and then tells them to get rid of them! As hard as this may be for you to do, especially if you are closely connected to the product or service or if it's something you have worked hard to create, you must let it go if it's not meeting sales goals.

After removing poorly performing products, the business owners on the show are then prompted by Lemonis to either create new ones that will sell better, or produce more of the currently available products or services that are selling the best. This frees up key assets like time, money, and energy, and redirects them toward potentially more profitable endeavors.

I recommend doing this with your team, if you have one. If you don't, recruit a person you trust to help; you need someone who is going to be real with you, and who can look at things objectively and not just tell you what you want to hear.

Keep in mind: you will review your own business biannually, and in the meantime, clients will review your business all year long. Thanks to Yelp, Google, and other online review opportunities, you'll enjoy continuous feedback (good and bad) from your customers.

I recommend getting out ahead of the reviews. Again, as I've said in prior chapters, pre-planning is key. Be the first to ask how a client's service was, or how they liked their product by sending out a review email. You're not done yet! Then you must take their feedback into account and become better as a result. If people give you a good review, send them links to your Yelp or Google page. If they rate you poorly, follow up by asking how you could have made the services better or what you can do to make it up to them.

Clients are less likely to comment negatively about your company when they see evidence of your concern for their experience. Feeling like they are already being heard and knowing you are willing to resolve their problems will prevent them from going to Yelp or Google to complain. If they can connect with a real person who cares and not consider your enterprise a faceless corporation, they will freely work with you to make sure their satisfaction level is high. This brings them into the process and gives them some measure of control.

> "Don't you worry your pretty little mind,
> people throw rocks at things that shine."
> – Taylor Swift

While you may get some incredible reviews, you will inevitably receive negative ones, too. These are the ones that sting—the ones you can dwell on for weeks, months, or years. Trust me, I've been there.

I planned and executed one of the most stunning weddings of my career—every detail was beautiful and exactly what the couple wanted at the most gorgeous resort. I felt prepared, knowledgeable, and on top of my game.

When it was all said and done, I received a scathing review from the Mother of the Groom. The bride and groom were head over heels with our service as was the bride's family. But the mother of the groom was unhappy with our service and how elaborate it was. I remember at one point during the planning process saying to the mother of the groom, "I just want everyone to be happy," and she replied with, "You can't please everyone, darling!" My jaw dropped. Then—to receive this review after the insanely gorgeous wedding they had—literally took my breath away.

Regardless, I took her criticism to heart and my heart felt like someone didn't approve of me. I carried that bad review with me to an international wedding conference, where I literally cried with another wedding planner (whom I didn't know before we sat next to each other at a cocktail party) about this woman's disapproval. It was a new low.

I felt like I had made a mistake somewhere along the way, like I had messed up. The truth is, her criticism had nothing to do with me.

At the same conference, I asked one of the senior event planners, "What's the worst thing that has ever happened to you at a wedding?"

He replied, "Oh, honey, let me tell you a story."

He went on to tell me about a wedding reception he'd planned for more than four hundred guests. It was held in a gorgeously draped tent lit by twenty-five grand chandeliers, with TV screens set into the dance floor and covered by protective glass. All of these centerpieces required electric power. On the big day, the unimaginable happened: the electricity went out.

The planner told his assistant where the generators where located. Instead of pushing the generator switch back up slowly, his assistant did it all at once, which blew the main fuse. One of the chandeliers came unplugged and toppled onto a guest on the dance floor, breaking her jaw and crashing through the glass floor into the televisions below. The planner was sued for over a hundred thousand dollars!

After hearing this story, I gained perspective. I should not be worried because the mother of the groom was upset that the flowers were too grand. She was actually right: you *can't* please everyone. I had done my best to satisfy the bride. It was to her I owed my allegiance. I had to let it go.

The truth is, in business as in life, you get to choose what you focus on. Putting unexpected bad reviews or general roadblocks into perspective will keep you from letting unfortunate occurrences direct your path forward. Learn from them, and move on.

Stop worrying! Start minding
your own business.

refine

Now that you've given yourself feedback and listened to the feedback of others (without letting it hurt you), it's time to refine your business.

What can you do that will make your operations just a bit better, and what parts can you completely transform? You have to step back and start to refine bits and pieces. When you get feedback, don't ignore it. Take it in, swish it around in your mouth, and if it's the truth, swallow it and begin to make changes. If it's untrue, spit it out and let it run down the drain, away and gone. You don't have to evaluate this part with anyone else—unless you want to. Your heart will tell you what's right. Taking a good long look at the areas we can refine or make better after we have reviewed is essential.

Everything you put out into the world needs to be polished just a little bit. While, these days, people value what's real, authentic, and raw, I still believe in polishing. Polish your content, polish your language, really think about the point you are trying to get across. Brainstorm all the ways you could say something, and then say it in the best possible way.

Conceptualize | Session #35
edit

> Edit. Edit. Edit.

These three words I like to apply, not only to business, but to every aspect of my life. Relentless editing is what makes *Vogue* magazine great. It's what makes your favorite book incredible. In another sense, it's what creates the aesthetic of your brand. It's what makes a home feel lovely and uncluttered. "Edit" runs on repeat in my head because there are so many things I love; activities I want to do; business ideas and décor items I want to create. I constantly have to stop and remind myself to edit. Content is so much better edited. So are SOPs. Narrow everything down to what is most needed, useful, and connecting. Get to the heart of the matter, the heart of the home, the heart of your business.

You have to edit. Just like lifestyle consultant Marie "Konmari" Kondo has told us to do with our homes—to only keep the things that "spark joy"—we also need to do this in our business. We must select the services and products that "spark joy"—and also spark profit, too. If not, then select a few things that spark joy for you, personally. While they may be part of your business, you must consider them your hobby. As my business coach reminded me many times, if it's not making a profit, it's a hobby. I have come to realize that it's okay to have hobbies. It doesn't have to be all about the profit unless you are considering it a "business." But bringing our personal sense of joy into our work can be quite valuable.

Vogue has to be edited to the ninth degree. Do you know how much content they are given for review every month? They have to edit hundreds of pages down to only what they consider to be the absolute best for the magazine. In the same way, we must edit our business: how many products or services are you currently offering, and do all of them make sense to bring to market?

I also suggest editing when it comes to your aesthetic. Once you have chosen the aesthetic that best represents your brand, stick with it. Compile many different touchpoints of your brand and look at them all together. Ask yourself: are they aligned? Are there any pieces that stick out as being "off brand" or not in harmony with the collective whole?

In the beginning of my enterprise, I wanted to share *everything* we did with the public, even if it didn't match our brand at all. I slowly realized this only confused people, instead of helping them understand what we excelled in. Make sure you only share photos or stories that match your brand and where you want it to go in the future. Where you are right now is great, but where you are going or what you are doing next is even better. If you share only the things you love doing, you will refine your client base to match your preferences.

> This is the power of editing: you can precisely and concisely highlight exactly what you want to show your customer.

Someone who is selling precious stones for a ring would overwhelm a customer if they showed twenty or more options all at once. Learning about the customer would enable them to narrow down to between three and five options. This personalizes the experience for the client, increasing the likelihood of a positive outcome.

You must edit the options to help them make a decision. So many times, it feels like we should give people more options to help fit their exact needs. In reality, however, we see that the fewer the choices provided, the more likely clients are to make a choice they are happy with.

Conceptualize | Session #36
get after it

Ask! All you have to do is ask. Don't take no for an answer. If you don't ask, the answer will most definitely be "no."

> "You can't use up creativity.
> The more you use, the more you have."
> –Oscar Wilde

Here is the hardest part for me: the only rule in business is—**there are no rules.** I wanted to make sure I was doing it correctly; I was worried for many years that I was doing business wrong. I came to find out, after hiring many business coaches and life coaches, there is no right or wrong way. There is merely how *you* can do it best, which is so hard.

I wanted these coaches to give me steps—the exact steps I needed to take to be successful. What I really needed to know was when to follow my heart and break the rules. The irony is, I am now writing a book with steps that will, hopefully, make you successful! Life can come full circle when you pay attention.

No one is going to give you permission to make the jump from your day job to your dream job. No one is going to give you permission to raise your prices. No one is going to give you permission to do anything that's good for your business. Why do we seek permission? It is ingrained in us.

> Forget permission. When there are obstacles, you have to jump!

Going after your dreams is never easy. That is why many don't succeed. You, my friend, are different. You want it. You want your dream so badly that you are willing to pursue it and push past the hard stuff.

I had a business coach once who challenged me on everything I wanted to do. I told him I wanted to go to France on an industry retreat for networking. He told me it wasn't a wise use of our profits. At first, I felt like he didn't believe in my abilities. After a few months of discussing it, I thought *maybe he cares so much that he wants me to focus on one region or area instead of expanding*. After a long call, he said he thought the trip to France was just a leisure trip and I couldn't turn it into a business opportunity. That was the moment I realized I should not be putting so much weight on his opinion.

> If I am going to bet on anyone, it's going to be myself.

I have gotten myself this far. Getting objective advice—from a coach or even from this book—is important, but in the end you must tailor it to your dreams and goals. If that involves rule breaking, so be it.

I took the trip to France. There, we stayed at a gorgeous château, and I ended up posting about the château and destination weddings on Instagram. Half an hour later, I got a call from a bride who wanted to get married at the château she had seen on Instagram! We not only booked our first French wedding, but I also made amazing connections on the trip that will last a lifetime.

Don't get me wrong: I believe in asking for advice. Always ask. You don't have to accept the answer or agree with it, but the more opinions you get, the more you understand other perspectives, the more your own limited view expands, and the more you are able to trust your instincts.

You know deep down in your gut what is right for you and for your business. If you believe you should do something, you should do it. If you are hesitating, there is probably a reason to hesitate. Gut feelings are built in to help us make tough decisions. We have to dig deep to find that gut intuition, and once you find it, you have to roll with it.

> "Don't ask for permission, demand it!"
> - Jasmine Star

Confidence is everything. Did you ever watch the show *The O.C.?*

If not, let me tell you a bit about it. *The O.C.* was broadcasted during one of the most formidable times of my life: high school. The major focus of character development for the main character, Seth Cohen, was confidence. He had none at the beginning of the show and, as the storyline develops, you watch him slowly gain confidence. He ends up winning the woman of his dreams, being able to help his troubled friend, and ultimately—grow into a deeply self-assured man.

I believe this is possible for all of us. We all have the opportunity to grow in confidence. As we do, both in life and business, we become more attractive. We carry ourselves differently. Confidence helps us stand out from our competition.

Brendon Burchard, author of *High Performance Habits*, believes in daily affirmations—the act of intentionally encouraging yourself. I not only have a daily pep talk I have posted in multiple places and say each day, but I also do what Brendon instructs us to do: I set my alarm multiple times a day. This works as a trigger to think about certain things and to focus on what I need to during that time.

It's essential that you write your own daily pep talk and read it to yourself every morning to start your day. It should be customized to you and your life and what you want out of the next twenty-four hours. Here's how:

Start with what you know about yourself. What do you believe about yourself? What characteristics do you possess? What do you need? What do you know is true about yourself that you sometimes need to be reminded of? Write it down.

I am …
I have …
I live in …

I'll share mine with you as an example of what you can create. As you can see, you are definitely allowed multiples of each pronouncement:

I am minding my own business.
I am creative.
I am brave.
I have an eye for style and design.
I am confident.
I live in truth.
I create beauty.
I am kind.
I am lovely.
I am smart.
I am inspiring.
I am grateful.
I am giving glory to God.
I am impeccable with my word.
I am not taking anything personally.
I am not making assumptions.
I am doing my very best.

I am light.
I am love.
I am honest.
I am tackling life & business head on.
I am dreaming big.
I am doing bigger.

Setting reminders (alarms on your phone or computer, or notes posted throughout your office) will trigger you to remember your pep talk, to act on the things you know, to be proactive, and to make sure you are checking in on your productivity. Are you accomplishing what you set out to do? Have you worked on your action steps for the day?

Go ahead: set up these processes, systems, and reminders in your business to review, refine, edit, and then get after it every three months. You will notice your business runs more efficiently, you'll become more confident, and your days will become more productive. Instead of getting stuck in the daily grind and whirlwind, you'll be able to constantly scale up your business. As you start to level up, you will need to put new standards in place; this is cyclical, and so beneficial to continuing the growth process. In this next chapter, you will set high standards for yourself and your life.

I promise, you will never look back.

No. 9

HIGH STANDARDS.

HIGH STANDARDS

"Keep your heels, head, and standards high!"
— Coco Chanel

It's time to set your standards. What will you *always* do? What will you *no longer* do?

Sometimes we learn lessons and then end up "learning" them again and again. Why is that? We seldom decide we are *always* going to or *never* going to do something, because it seems so final. However—once we've learned a lesson—I think it's imperative that we set standards and non-negotiables. This is how we continue to improve.

"Fool me once, shame on you; fool me twice, shame on me."
—George Horne

We have to make our non-negotiable list and then stick to it, as hard as it may be. This helps us avoid making the same mistake twice and narrows our focus to what is most needed and valuable. It helps us decide from the start where we want to put our energy, instead of trying to focus on everything at once.

My team and I have new clients do this at the beginning of their wedding planning process. What is non-negotiable for your wedding? We had one couple whose list was:

- Must have our dog, Sadie, in the wedding
- Must have a dessert bar filled with all kinds of delectable treats
- Must have an In-N-Out truck for late-night snacks

How sweet, right? We love this process, but often forget to do it for our own life and business.

On a personal note, after spending four days with my extended family at the age of thirty-two, I began to realize sometimes it is important to say, **"Enough is enough."** I don't know about you, but I come from a family where things are done a certain way simply because they have always been done that way. Standards are important, but they can and do change along with circumstances and new ideas.

When my mother and father grew up, their families' rule was that "children are to be seen and not heard." Kids were not listened to, nor were their opinions brought into account. And they were definitely not included or informed about decisions being made. And when I say "children," I mean even those over the age of eighteen. If they were the offspring of the older generation, they were still treated as children and not given respect as the adults they had grown to become. In my opinion, treating them as children makes them act like children (even if they are not). I understand this was the generational norm, but they continued to live by those standards. How sad that this mentality has persisted in how they raise *their* family.

Every year, on Christmas Day, instead of enjoying dinner as a family—having everyone share what they are grateful for and having a true family discussion—the "older generation" speaks, and the "children" are told to be quiet and listen. Instead of including them and setting the bar high for them, standards are set as low as when they were toddlers. They acted as if the "children" were not even at the table—which makes younger but mature people just want to leave the table, and act as children.

Why not set the standards high? Believe in the kids, let them state their opinions, inform them, discuss, and spend time as a family. A lifetime of family dinners like this made me see that this dynamic was not beneficial for anyone. Now don't get me wrong; I believe in respecting our elders. But I also think that we should respect our children, showing by example our high standards for them and giving them the chance to be heard. After all, they will be adults one day, and must practice acting with maturity.

Why stick with the old, unequal model just because it's been done that way for years? Sometimes people do things a certain way for years until it becomes a tradition. And traditions are often considered high standards by virtue of their longevity, when this may not be the case at all—and actually, may in fact be the opposite. So, in life and in business, we really need to evaluate and set standards that are beneficial—not just traditional.

After a long discussion with a cousin, I came to see things are not going to change until we stand up and say, **"Enough is enough."** It's time to break with a hollow tradition and, in this case, form new ways of sharing the holidays with our own families. The same is true of business.

> Keep what works, recognize what doesn't serve you any longer, and move on... always setting the bar high.

One business standard we have adopted in my company is to only plan a wedding twelve months prior to the actual date. We can book the venue sooner, but the actual detailed planning process needs to commence no sooner than twelve months out. It's a quality-control issue. This prevents clients from changing their minds to succumb to tempting new trends and styles over the course of more than a year. We can serve them best if we agree on event goals and themes, with a no-turning-back cutoff point.

There is one specific example that set this high standard in stone. We had started planning for a client three years prior to the wedding (yes, they had a three-year engagement).

After planning everything for them during year one, the bride not only changed her idea of *what* she wanted for her wedding, she also changed her mind about the *groom*. She called off the entire wedding and wanted us to ask for all of her deposits back. Because the wedding was still so far off, many of the vendors were okay with forfeiting the deposit; they could still easily take on other projects. But what about Couture Events? My team and I had already done the work of planning *the entire wedding*—and now had to do the work of *undoing* the entire wedding. We didn't get our final payment, and the "bride" even wanted our deposit back.

To my detriment, I let a similar scenario happen a handful of times before I implemented the rule: twelve months at most. This is a lesson learned, which became a new standard.

Of course, some standards are no-brainers; we know we need them without having to learn the lesson the hard way. To find mine, I asked myself, "What standards do I live by and want to bring into my business?" I came up with ten golden standards that have persisted at our company for the last ten years and are given to each of our coordinators when they begin with us:

1. **Love**

   Everything we do is rooted in *love*. The love of love. Love for each other, our clients, and love of weddings and designing.

2. **Honesty**

   For my team and those we work with I ask that everyone be honest with me about how you are doing with things, how you feel about the events you are planning and projects you are working on, how you feel about where you are in life, what you want to do, and what you don't want to do. *No lies (even if they are white)*. Complete honesty, one hundred percent of the time. Communication is *key!*

   You can make a million dollar mistake but if you are honest about it, we can work through it.

3. **Integrity**

What do you do when no one is watching? Have integrity for the brand and yourself. You know what is right. *Do it,* and make sure it's being done for your clients.

4. **Our Family**

We treat our business like a family. We believe in keeping the same values we have at home in business:

- Trust
- Teamwork
- Solidarity
- Loyalty

5. **Couture Service**

We are a high-end event coordination company, tailoring the event to the client. We specialize in custom services. We have a servant's heart, helping clients through every step, remembering this may be their first time getting married. Go above and beyond for the client and vendors we love, push the envelope. Customer service is dead... it's all about customer *love!* This means:

- We pay for the clients' meals
- We bring them coffee
- We attend to their needs
- We answer all emails within forty-eight hours

- We *never* just forward an email (we explain it to the client or summarize it for them, as well as forward)
- We always address them by name in an email
- We answer our phones whenever possible and have on our outgoing voicemail messages, "Hello, this is _____ with Couture Events."
- Instagram and Facebook are a part of our brand. Our personal Instagram feeds reflect on our business.

6. **Quality**

We want quality clients.

We have quality vendors.

We make sure quality is given to the clients in every aspect.

We *PRODUCE QUALITY.*

7. **Respect**

Respect the client, respect the vendors, and respect yourself.

No disrespect is allowed. We do not talk about our vendors, each other, or our clients poorly for any reason while at work or when working together. If you need to, get someone outside of our company with whom you can "vent," because it will not be happening here. Our workplace is a positive environment. *Good vibes only!*

8. **Creativity**

    We must think on our feet and be creative with our solutions to problems and the ways in which we deliver them.

9. **Beauty**

    We believe that beauty comes from the inside out. Be beautiful on the inside, and others will be attracted to you because of that... and you will shine on the outside.

> "If you have good thoughts, they will shine out of your face like sunbeams, and you will always look lovely"
> —Roald Dahl

10. **The Best**

    It's the best, or nothing! No exceptions.
    Strive for perfection; be happy with the attempt.

Conceptualize | Session # 37
high standards

Take the time to write out what is most important to you about your business. What do you want your employees to know, and what should they do, no matter what?

After writing out your standards, think about the little things that will help you get there. Write them out as *I will always* or *I will never*. It feels very final, but it's actually really good to create boundaries around your life and business.

For me:

- I will ALWAYS respond to clients within forty-eight hours. I go a little crazy when it takes someone longer than that to get back to me, so I want to treat our clients with the same respect I would want.

- I will ALWAYS put all correspondence with clients into written form and send via email. Even if it's a phone call, I will do an email recap. I want to make sure we are on the same page, and details are clearly listed out, so we can look back at the conversation we just had, with the details in writing.

- I will NEVER share anything about my personal life with clients before their event. They do not want or need to know about my great aunt Sally having surgery or that my dog just had puppies. I keep my personal life separate from my professional life with the client.

- I will ALWAYS hold my family and home as sacred ground. I don't invite clients over to my home or invite them out to meet my family. For some, doing that might be okay (maybe you love entertaining at your home, and that is wonderful), but for me—my home is my safe space. In my job, I plan everyone else's life and almost every moment of their day. I am constantly "on." I don't want to get home and entertain. I want to come home and relax and enjoy my family. The time I get with them is special.

- I will NEVER answer a client call when I am at home with my little one. I don't think it's respectful to my daughter—or to my client.

- I will ALWAYS be present. When I am at home, I will be at home. When I am at work, I will be at work. This is the best way I have found to split the time and not have the mom/wife guilt or boss guilt. I have to separate the two spheres, and for me that works. I don't bring my family to work events. I do not to bring work home with me.

Setting standards takes gumption. It takes a lot of bravery to say, "To heck with it, I'm just going to do what I think is right for us."

> Nothing great ever happened without a little conviction.

You have to take a stand, as I did in moving away from the old family model for holidays. If you don't, it will never happen.

Some honest discussion prepares us for setting high standards. If you asked each family member, for instance, what their dream holiday looked like, you might get a lot of different answers—or you might find you had more in common than you thought. Suppose you found out, after all of these years, you really all wanted the same thing but no one wanted to say it! It's time to take that family cruise you've all been dreaming of. Having high standards means defining how you live your life, *and why.*

I am an idealist. I always want to believe the best about people, and perhaps even that they are better than they really are. I imagine they are deeper, kinder, and better than I can see on the surface. I hope and pray this part of them will come out and show up. Many times I am disappointed, but for the few yet distinct times I wasn't, it was worth it. The old adage says, "expect nothing and then you'll never be disappointed"—but I can't live like that.

I have decided to paint my own positive reality. I live with my head in the clouds and my feet on the ground. I celebrate the tiny victories. I get excited over the details. I believe in God (even though I don't fully understand why things happen the way they do). I believe in love and fairy tales. I call a spade a spade, and I mean what I say. I choose to see people as beautiful, lovely, kind, and fabulous—and if they disappointment me, so be it. At least I believed in them.

I have worked very hard in my life to make others proud, but it's deeper than that. It's to make *myself* proud. Proud of who I am, and proud of being able to stand behind my actions and words. If I don't win the approval of those I want to make proud, but I have stayed true to myself and what I know to be true, my high standards are still worth it. Join me in this lifelong effort. After all, I believe in you!

Chapter
ten

RULES

TO

LIVE

BY

RULES TO LIVE BY

> *"You know all of those things you have always wanted to do? You should do them."*
> —Unknown

This is it: the final chapter. I know I told you at times I prefer to push the rules, but it is often in service of *improving* upon old or ill-fitting mandates—not to promote anarchy. I have spent considerable time thinking over and devising guidelines for my life and business based on what's beneficial to the most people at a given time. Things change. Traditions fade away. New structures must take their place.

In this chapter, I will leave you with rules to live by that will help you through your journey of designing this life you love and then taking action. The following rules are not just "ideals," they are *ways to live, ways to love,* and *ways to run your business.* We have to lay down rules by which we will abide, so we can be free in other areas. We also do it to respect the boundaries of others.

> If you don't set out on this adventure of life with rules, you will fall short and end up in someone else's way, or on someone else's path.

People take the "easy" route when they don't make a plan to get where they are going. They don't reevaluate their methods as times change, because it's easier to go with what once worked. That won't get you any closer to living the life of your dreams. The rules that brought you to where you are now may not be able to lead you to where you want to go. It's like taking a road trip. You *must* know your current location and look forward to crossing what lies between you and your destination if you want to succeed on your journey.

As I look to the future of entrepreneurship, I know things will change drastically in the next ten years. Culture, technology, and humankind are advancing quickly. The world will quite literally look very different ten years from now than it currently does. We must both stay in the moment and keep that future in mind.

Some of the strongest advice I've ever received was from Duncan Wardle, former Director of Creativity and Innovation at Disney. Wardle is a businessman through and through; he has been at the top of the corporate ladder, and has seen so much more than most people will ever get to see in life and in business. When I was able to interview him for our CONFETTI podcast, he showed up to be interviewed—barefoot. When I asked why he was barefoot, he replied, "Why not?" We were at a beachside resort in Cabo San Lucas, yet most people were wearing shoes. Not Duncan. I could sense that, despite his success—or perhaps, *because of it*—he has learned to not take things too seriously. He is clearly a man who strives to live every moment and seize every opportunity. When talking about the future of business and technology, he acknowledged, "Everything will be programmed. Technology will overtake us," he said. "But here is where we, as small business entrepreneurs and humankind, will be able to compete:

1. Creativity

2. Imagination

3. Intuition

4. Curiosity

"You can't program these things," he assured me. "These four skill sets we are born with are going to become the most important."

Terrifying. But, exciting.

In reality, how do I think this will look? Computers will know more than us, and we won't be able to compete with their knowledge. Artisans and creatives and businesspeople alike will have access to 3D printers and will be able to "make anything." There won't be as many handmade treasures. Their scarcity will render these objects— these crafts—and the people who make them more meaningful. They will have greater value. By being forced to go back to the four basics that Wardle described, we will in some ways, return to our own roots. It begs the question: *what makes us people?*

This brings us full circle to the beginning of this book, when I encouraged you to find and name your purpose. This purpose is what will make you different. It will help you stand out, and even as time progresses and technology becomes more prevalent, it's the one thing you can capitalize on in life and in your business. Our uniqueness is the soul of who we are—the soul of who we were created to be. Our very being has these creative skill sets embedded in it, and that's why I believe our purpose in life is so much deeper than what we do for a living. Yes, work *is* a big part of it—but not all.

> Your real purpose is minding your own business,
> figuring out who you are, and using your
> unique gifts to lead yourself to success.

Are you that inquisitive person? "She" minds her own business and defines her own success when she gets back to the basics of what makes her soul purposeful.

RULE #1:
THE FUTURE WILL ALWAYS BE DIFFERENT

Conceptualize | Session #38
future of business

172

When forced to use our creativity, imagination, intuition, and curiosity again, which skills will you embrace and bring with you to the future? As an entrepreneur, if you can build your business around any of these four things, you will likely continue to flourish and have sustainability for the next decade and beyond.

By developing brands, businesses, and lives that are meaningful and rich in creativity, we'll have a pretty good handle on the future. With each page of this book, you have started to design your life and your business in such a way. Now it's time to hold on tight and make sure you stay true to yourself.

Somewhere along the road of your life, it's likely someone has broken you down. Maybe someone once told you the rocket ship you imagined you were playing in was just a cardboard box. Or that you're not creative enough, or that your curiosity is annoying. You may have stopped believing in yourself or practicing those four skills you were born with. Now it's time to bring back those skills into your life, practice them daily, and apply them to your core strengths.

Take a look at the convictions you've made while working with this book. Recall who, besides yourself, will hold you accountable for pursuing them. Now, project yourself ten, twenty, thirty years into the future. Your innate skills are what will keep you on track toward your goals during that time. Think of ways you can use them *right now* to meet your standards and make progress toward your goals.

RULE #2:
PROFIT FIRST

For me the largest issues in my business have always surrounded finances. While I am not a financial expert, I felt that adding this rule was essential. As business owners we are always on a journey of learning, but this rule is one I wish I would have known and implemented from the start. I must also state that this is not a value (I don't value profit first in my company; it's a principle, or a rule, that we run our business by.)

Looking back I have had three recurring problems in my business:

1. Reinvestment: Because I love what I do, I always see the potential in reinvesting in my business. So when is enough, enough? There will always be more I could do, spend, and invest in my business and I want to build the business of my dreams BUT—it is a business that needs to make a profit.

2. Payment and motivation for my TRIBE: those who work for us, such as independent contractors or employees. I want to invest in them monetarily and when I first started, I over-invested (more than what I should have) because I wanted to make sure they felt compensated correctly—without looking at the expenses incurred. For example, I paid our contractors a percentage of the package they booked but didn't take out/think about expenses first. So while we promised forty percent, once we deducted our expenses (office space, marketing money, gifting for our clients, retreats for our team, etc.) they were actually making more like eighty percent. We then had to redo our payment structure by first outlining and removing our expenses, and then giving a percentage based on the new bottom line. This was rough because I had been over-compensating them, but then had to take away some of their payment to make sure the business was profitable. I would suggest you start lower and you can always give raises rather than having to subtract pay. In addition, because I was trying to build our team and constantly reinvest, I wasn't taking payment for myself—this is a slippery slope.

3. Taxes: After graduating from college, getting a degree in communications and a minor in public relations, and working for a corporation, I started my own business and thought I understood taxes. During the fifth year of my business, my husband called to say our taxes were complete and that the tax person said we owed eighteen hundred dollars… or at least that's what I heard. I returned home and as we were in the midst of running out the door to have dinner with friends I wrote the check and handed it to him… and he handed it right back.

"Honey, we don't owe eighteen hundred dollars," he said. "We owe eighteen thousand."

Excuse me, WHAT?! How was this even possible? I didn't have that much money; I feel like I barely even made that much. The questions continued to swirl in my head, followed by the accusations: I went to college; I should know how to calculate my taxes. I felt so ashamed; why didn't I understand this?

Tears rolled down my face as I thought, "this business was supposed to make me money and now, it has put me in debt." How would I ever come up with this money? I started to cry, then sob.

Despite how much my husband tried to comfort me, I just had to get out of there. I put on my sweats and took off running (and mind you, I don't run). I took off with no direction in mind, but as

I ran I thought someone should have warned me about this—to set aside my taxes as I made the money. I wanted someone to blame, so I started running in the direction of my college. I wanted to talk to my professors; why wasn't the topic of taxes on any test?

I continued to run, thoughts swirling, when my husband pulled up beside me in the car and said, "Honey, it's okay, get in. We will figure it out."

Now looking back on this sad but true story, I realize it was my own ignorance—and not the people around me—that had gotten me to this point. I had ignored the taxes myself because it was "scary" and I didn't understand it, but once I was forced to come face-to-face with the reality of understanding taxes, I knew I needed to make a plan.

I wish I would have known then about the book *Profit First* by Mike Michalowicz. I advise you to read his book to get a deeper understanding of his philosophy, but the overall idea is this:

As business owners we've defaulted to taking out profits once we've paid our expenses. But Michalowicz recommends this: Bi-monthly (or in our case as each paycheck comes in from our clients), take percentages out and put them into separate accounts for profit, taxes, owners' compensation, and then expenses/operations. Instead of keeping one large account that you pay everything from and putting everything into or taking out your expenses first—what if you took the profit first; accounted for the taxes; paid yourself and only then used what was left over?

I know this is so backwards from what we learned in school and in life but it makes so much more sense. If we operate by taking out our expenses first, then there could very well be nothing left when it comes to profit, taxes, or compensation. As a principle we will spend what we have. I truly believe this. I have learned from our brides, whether it be a $10k or $100k budget, they will spend the full budget they have. The same is true in life and business, you spend what you have "available" to you unless you divvy it out correctly before seeing what is "available".

Danielle Mulvey, helped me better understand this principle when we invited her to speak at Confetti Conference. When we have less to spend, we will make the most out of what we have. So by taking out our profit, taxes, and owners' compensation first, we will then use what is left over on expenses. We will make it work because we have to. This might mean re-evaluating our expenses and seeing where we can cut down or realizing the way we are currently operating isn't working and we need to completely restructure. This is okay; if it needs to be done, do it now. Don't ignore it.

This became a new rule in our business: to operate according to the *Profit First* philosophy and to ensure that our business is first and foremost profitable. We now set our profit percentage so we know exactly what our profit is, and when we say we can give ten percent of our profits, we know we'll have the profits to give. When I made Karina a profit-share partner, I knew at the end of the year exactly how much she would get—because we set the profit aside throughout the year to make this possible. Your first few years in business you might make less profit, and may only be able to set aside five percent or so. But the more you grow, the leaner you'll get with your expenses, resulting in a growing profit over time.

I want you to be profitable; to see a return on your efforts, and to grow your business. I don't want you to fall into the same financial pressures I did, which is why I've designated this as a rule to live by.

RULE #3:
KNOWING YOURSELF IS THE MOST POWERFUL TOOL YOU HAVE

Conceptualize | Session #39
enneagram

> "Knowing yourself is the beginning of all wisdom."
> —Aristotle

When you begin to understand yourself on a deeper level, you'll realize why you make the decisions you do, lead the way you do, or what you are naturally drawn to do. This self-realization gives you insight into how you relate to others, and how they relate to you—and it gives you the power to influence those relationships, not just react to them. You can use what drives and motivates you to get the best of any given situation.

Self-knowledge also helps you remove your own lens, when needed, to see situations from a more abstract, unbiased, or empathetic perspective. Do you need to let go of old habits? Tamp down your emotions to get at hard truths? Put yourself in someone else's shoes to solve a problem with them? Most of us resist these efforts, in part because we don't see ourselves as we truly are.

The tool that has been the most helpful for me in getting to know myself has been the enneagram. If you aren't familiar with this personality gauge, take time to identify your enneagram type and number. There are many tests, but my preferred one is at www. enneagramtest.net. It will tell you a lot about how you think and feel in relation to how others do.

I have used this test for myself, my team, and even my family. Knowing the enneagram number of your tribe members enables you to better understand their individual needs, assets, and liabilities. In each part of my life, and specifically in my business, this emotional-quotient identifier has been a game changer. It has helped me understand how to best utilize each member of my team and assign them to their sweet spot.

The test will not only help you determine your weaknesses, but it will also provide solutions for turning them into strengths. There are motivations for our own behaviors that are sometimes difficult for us to see; revealing your truths through this test is eye-opening. In fact, some of my team members felt a little bit *too* "seen."

> Owning up to your own weaknesses and vulnerabilities takes its own kind of strength.

But it pays off: this test is challenging in the best way. It has been pretty much spot on for us. Use it to get to know yourself and those around you better.

RULE #4:
CREATE AND KEEP
AGREEMENTS WITH YOURSELF

Conceptualize | Session #40
the four agreements

Years ago, I was at the back of the line in a bank. At the front of the line, a conversation was underway between two friends. The woman was going on and on about another friend, not currently present, who "needed help" and "didn't have her act together." She continued to tell the man about this woman who was, obviously, having a hard time in life.

Instead of joining the woman in her critique, the man said, "Oh, she needs to read and commit to *The Four Agreements*... and I think they would be good for you, too." I took note that he didn't get involved, he didn't gossip, or even respond, "Oh, I'm sorry to hear that." I eavesdropped and wrote down "*The Four Agreements*" in my phone notes. Later that night, I looked them up.

Don Miguel Ruiz introduces the concept of making an in-depth pact with ourselves in his great book entitled, *The Four Agreements*. Regardless of your personal beliefs and background, his advice—based on ancient Toltec writings—applies. It is not only universal but transformational. Ready?

The Four *agreements*

1. **Be impeccable with your word.**
   Ruiz says this means speaking intentionally, not frivolously. You strive to say what you mean. You don't denigrate yourself or others. You use the power of speech positively, to bring truth and love to those listening.

2. **Don't take anything personally.**
   Understand that people act on their own accord, not in relation to you. Resist the urge to be defensive without evidence. Even negative words or actions are a projection of an individual's psyche.

3. **Don't make assumptions.**
   Be brave enough to question people's motives, and to let them know what yours are. This will help you better connect and prevent misunderstanding, hurt feelings, and misplaced retaliation. This step alone will improve all of your relationships.

4. **Always do your best.**
   We are not constantly at our peak, but we *can* always strive to do our best in the moment. Remember the chronotypes Daniel Pink taught us about? Your energy and abilities fluctuate—at different times of the day, and in different circumstances. Don't worry that you might have performed better on another day, or if you didn't have a cold, or had slept better the night before. Just do the best you can, and you'll have no regrets.

You can dig deeper into these agreements and find out for yourself how they will affect your life. If you flip back to my daily pep talk in Chapter 8, you will see a new connection. I wrote The Four Agreements into it. I firmly believe these four agreements will make a world of difference in my everyday life. I sincerely believe they can do the same for you.

The hardest agreements for me to stick with are *"don't take anything personally,"* and *"don't make assumptions."* We do these things because: a) we tend to be self-absorbed, seeing things only from our perspective; and b) assumptions are shortcuts that save us thinking time. As soon as I was consciously aware of these fallback habits and ways of thinking, I realized that almost every day I took things personally or made assumptions. Now, I separate myself from others' opinions by realizing I have no idea what is going on in someone else's life or why they are acting the way they are. But I can ask.

> Perspective is everything.

Each person is at a different place in their lives and has a different focus. I was recently at a business club where I knew a lot of people in the room, but they didn't know each other. One man sat at a table, talking to an investor about contributing a hundred thousand dollars to his cause. Another man had a TV show and was looking for people to feature on it. There was a woman who'd just found the sister she had never known she had—she was adopted and didn't know she had a full-blood sister—and was getting ready to meet her the next day. There was a million-dollar deal about to happen, and someone else wanted to have a baby. The latter was a woman who was having infertility problems, and she couldn't think about anything else—even though she was in the room for business.

You never know what's going on in someone's life sitting next to you or across the table. Don Miguel Ruiz is right: we project on others what's on our minds. Usually, whatever you're currently focused on, you believe others are thinking about, too. The man with the TV show was talking to the woman who wanted a baby and was getting nowhere. He had no idea what was going on in her life and didn't ask. He assumed she would definitely want to be on television. The woman who'd just found out she had a sister was talking to the man who was about to make a million-dollar deal. This guy couldn't even hear what she was saying because he was focused on the magnitude of his business transaction.

It can be hard or impossible to connect when we make assumptions. And when we don't connect, we often take it personally. I wished I could have told everyone in the room what was really happening, letting them in on the secrets I knew about each of them. But we don't always talk about those things in public. So how do you get on the same page? You broaden your perspective.

Before, I used to make assumptions because I didn't want to ask questions, and I didn't want to dig any deeper. I took things at face value instead of asking the simple question, "*Why?*" I now discover so much more about where people are coming from and am able to get to the heart of real issues. Before I make up my mind or get defensive, I attempt to put the exchange in perspective.

I went to Malawi, Africa the summer before college. I spent three weeks there working with Children of the Nations in orphanages and poor villages. We are talking mud huts and straw roofs. I went to help, serve, and love on them, and while I hope I did those things I didn't expect to learn so much, myself. Every day was eye opening—a new lesson in perspective and worldview.

When I arrived at one of the orphanages the girls were playing with sticks and the boys with UNO cards. They had some books but that was it—sticks, books, and UNO. The very next day, a package arrived from a previous volunteer group that had visited this orphanage and the highlight of the package was a Barbie doll for each girl. I watched as they looked at the dolls, which they had never seen before, in the boxes. They ripped them out and started playing with the Barbies, but within thirty minutes the girls had started fighting over the different clothes and accessories that came with each doll. The most sought-after accessory quickly became the brush and they started pushing each other to try to get it. They then started fighting over the dolls themselves, with the older girls trying to take the dolls from the younger ones. It turned very ugly, very fast, and my heart broke.

The volunteers who sent the package had the intention of sending something "special" to the girls, yet it only brought greed and frustration. In fact, the girls were happier when they were playing with sticks.

Despite the group's intentions, I realized how misguided our worldviews truly can be. Not only did the Barbie dolls cause issues at the orphanage; they also caused problems in the village—not to mention, the dolls sent didn't even resemble the children in the least.

Perspective is everything. What if, instead of assuming, we took a step to ask?

Of course, we're not always free to ask questions. But we are free to respond reasonably, based on what we know. Ultimately, I give the benefit of the doubt. Then I mind my own business.

Inspired by *The Four Agreements*, I later added some of my own. Writing your own rules to live by is a crucial exercise to staying true to your path. I hope you'll do the same. Create agreements that you need in your life and follow them daily.

My four additional agreements to live by are:

1. **Be Kind.**

   There is never a reason not to be kind. Being kind means extending the benefit of the doubt, not drawing false conclusions, and turning the other cheek. After all—that's how you want to be treated, right?

2. **Be Honest.**

   The art of being tactfully honest is marked with sincerity and integrity. I don't believe in being rudely honest or "not having a filter." You're not required to speak out or respond with your opinion. But when I choose to speak, I believe in being truthful.

> "Then you will know the truth,
> and the truth will set you free."
> —John, 8:32

3. **Live Boldly.**

   Have the confidence to live boldly. If you know you are doing what is right and good, be confident with that certainty. You can live more intentionally because you have the confidence to do so. You can deliver with excellence because it's who you are. Be bold!

4. **Don't Compare.**

   Comparison is the thief of all joy. You will most certainly fail if you are comparing yourself to others, because you can't be exactly like them. You can only succeed if you are doing *you*. Instead of comparing, try encouraging and supporting. We're all in this together.

Those are my agreements. Now go write and live out yours! The results will be supremely satisfying.

Remember this?

"She" is an entrepreneur who designed her life and loved every inch of it.

She was not worried about what "they" were doing or how they defined success.

She didn't listen to what they had to say because she wasn't doing it for "them."

She set her own standards and priorities.

She pursued her goals and lived life to its fullest potential.

She kept her head in the clouds and her feet on the ground.

She stayed focused on the *joie de vivre,* celebrating the joy of life with each and every tiny victory.

My hope is that "she" is now **you.**

———————

#SheMindsHerOwnBusiness

That's you! You did it! You have done the work and the soul searching. You have made new commitments to yourself and your business. You have designed your dream life and business. Now it's time for you to go live it and OWN IT!

This is a lifelong quest. With plenty of work ahead of you and so much goodness in store, here are my final words of encouragement:

Take it one step at a time.

Give yourself grace.

Remember to breathe—great things come with time.

Keep the gorgeous end in mind, always.

It's not always easy, but the best things in life never are. Think of all the entrepreneurs who started with nothing but a dream. They overcame obstacles and kept at it—and some even made it far enough to write their own tickets and give interviews barefoot in the sand. From adversity comes the greatest successes. To that I would add: **and when we succeed... we celebrate!** I'll be with you, cheering you on. I know how far you've come.

Now, get out there. Go mind your own business! You've definitely got this.

To live is the rarest thing in the world.
Most people exist, that is all.
—Oscar Wilde

meet krystel

I so wish I could grab a latte with each of you in person at your favorite coffee shop. Instead we will have to meet on Instagram or at one of our live events.

You can find me @KrystelStacey and join our community by using our hashtag #SheMindsHerOwnBusiness. We would also love for you to join our Facebook Community: She Minds Her Own Business, where I share weekly inspiration and you can ask questions in a safe community of like-minded women.

I would also love to send you some encouraging & thoughtful words directly to your inbox each week.

You can subscribe at SheMindsHerOwnBusiness.com where you can also find a list of our live events.

I can't wait to meet you.

about the author

Krystel Stacey is a creative entrepreneur, author, speaker and vision strategist for business leaders. She is the founder of design & planning companies @CoutureEvents and @CocoandWhim, as well as @Confetti.Inc, a community for creative entrepreneurs.

With over a decade of experience growing three thriving businesses, Krystel is dedicated to inspiring fellow leaders and entrepreneurs through her successes, and her struggles. She has been recognized as a leader in her field and nominated Woman of the Year by San Diego Magazine.

Krystel's work has been featured on Huffington Post, Martha Stewart Weddings, Brides Magazine, and The Knot. She resides with her husband, daughter, and pup in Coronado, CA where she is inspired by the sunshine and the sea.

Krystel operates off the belief that this life is a gift and you only get one chance to live it, so you must go after your dreams full force. May this book in your hands—and your continued conversations with this community online—lead you to design the life and business you've always imagined!

Made in the USA
Middletown, DE
28 August 2022